IMAGES OF SCOTLAND

GLASGOW EAST

IMAGES OF SCOTLAND

GLASGOW EAST

GORDON ADAMS

The History Press

Dedicated with love to Gary for his birthday, 2007.

Frontispiece: Glasgow Cathedral, *c.* 1886.

First published in 2007
Reprinted 2012

The History Press
The Mill, Brimscombe Port,
Stroud, Gloucestershire, GL5 2QG
www.thehistorypress.co.uk

British Library Cataloguing in Publication Data.
A catalogue record for this book is available from the British Library.

ISBN 978 0 7524 4567 0

Typesetting and origination by
The History Press
Printed and bound in Great Britain by
Marston Book Services Limited, Didcot

Contents

Acknowledgements

I should like to thank everyone who has contributed towards the production of this book, particularly Gary O'Connor, and the following for allowing me to reproduce photographic material:

A.G. Barr PLC, 69b; Gerry Blaikie, 83b; Robert Bruce (Caledonian Breweries) and Iain Russell (Glasgow University Archives), 14t, 14b, 19t; Robert Bryson, 62b; Tim Buxbaum, 108b; Gordon Dinnie, 106b; Father Docherty, 106t; Anthony Duda, 12t, 12b, 13t, 26t, 26b, 33t, 42t, 51t, 51b, 52b, 53t, 54t, 56t, 56b, 57b, 58t, 58b, 59t, 61t, 65b, 67t, 67b, 72t, 72b, 73t, 74t, 78t, 81b, 83b, 85b, 86t, 86b, 92t, 122t; Enda Ryan (Glasgow City Libraries), 16t, 16b, 22b, 24b, 27t, 27b, 30t, 30b, 31t, 31b, 32t, 33b, 38t, 38b, 44t, 44b, 55t, 55b, 57t, 60b, 63t, 63b, 64t, 70t, 77t, 77b, 84b, 98b, 101t, 110t, 110b, 113t, 113b, 119t. 128t, 128b; Glasgow University, 45b; Ray Laycock, 76t, 76b; Nostalgia Cards, 119b; John Mackay (Shettleston Harriers), 75t, 116t, 121t; John O'Donnell, 53b; Elspeth McKissock and Margaret Wilson (Carmyle Reminiscence Group), 105t, 105b, 107t, 107b, 108t; Alex Richardson (Gladiator Program), 121b; Rutherglen Museum, 40b, 91b; Robert Birrell and Gregor Cameron (Sandyhills Golf Club), 79t; Scottish Conservation Projects, 102b; William A.C. Smith, 59b, 75b, 122b, 123b; Jim Thomson, 88t; Graham Twidale, 20b, 88b, 127b; David Warrilow, 45t.

My apologies to any copyright holders which I was unaware of and have not included attribution.

Selected Bibliography

Adams, Gordon (1990): *A History of Bridgeton & Dalmarnock*. Hill & Hay Ltd., Glasgow.
Adams, Gordon (1992): *A History of Tollcross & Dalbeth*. Clydeside Press, Glasgow.
Fisher, Joe (1994): *The Glasgow Encyclopedia*. Mainstream Publishing, Edinburgh and London
Waugh, Thomas (1986); *Shettleston from Old and New Photographs*. Heatherbank Press, Milngavie.
Williamson et al (1990); *Buildings of Scotland – Glasgow*. Penguin Books.
Wilson, Margaret (*c.* 1992); *Carmyle Recollections*. Carmyle Reminiscence Group, Glasgow.

www.EastGlasgowHistory.com provides an extensive and growing record of the area's history.

Introduction

There is seldom a single, correct way to define boundaries which everybody agrees with because these tend to be rather temporary, artificial and arbitrary creations; often dependent upon the location of a stream, a hedge, or a wall or even a pre-existing tradition where actual landmarks are missing. I have divided this book on east Glasgow into six sections, each comprised of a number of districts. I am conscious that some readers, understandably proud of their origins, will wonder why their particular district was included in one section rather than another. I fully acknowledge that this is essentially an idiosyncratic grouping undertaken for practical purposes because I also recognise this to be a perennial difficulty in presenting a local history book.

Where is east Glasgow anyway? That depends upon time and perspective. At the beginning of its recorded history the concept of an east Glasgow would have seemed a ridiculous notion to inhabitants who could see from one end of their community to the other. Much later, identification with a particular area of the city became, and remains, fiercely defended. Residents of some districts such as Tollcross and Baillieston, which have been more recently included within the city, still resist the very notion of being part of Glasgow at all, while in other districts people can hardly conceive of being anything else, while still retaining loyalty to their own district of birth. For the purposes of this book I have taken my demarcation line for east Glasgow to include everything enclosed to the east of a line running up Saltmarket, High Street and Castle Street from the Clyde to the M8 motorway. From there, it runs eastwards to Cumbernauld Road, following that route to the city limits. It then runs southwards to the Clyde and returns westwards to its beginning. This reflects my personal view of east Glasgow and provides a starting point for a consideration of its history!

For most of that known history, what is now east Glasgow belonged to the Catholic Church. Tradition has it that the early Celtic Christian missionary, St Ninian, was active in the fourth century in the area which was to become Glasgow. When St Mungo, who is credited with being the first Bishop of Glasgow, arrived in the sixth century, he took possession of a burial ground which St Ninian had consecrated. This was the core around which the extensive domain of his successors accumulated. As the Roman Catholic Church gained in ascendancy from the twelfth century onwards, donations of land were made by the laity to support its clergy. This land provided sustenance either from direct cultivation, animal husbandry or from rental to others. It is estimated that the Church eventually came to own fully a quarter of all Scotland!

When the feudal system was introduced, largely by King David I in the twelfth century, the bishops of the Church also became feudal lords. The medieval Bishops of Glasgow eventually held several lordships throughout the south of Scotland. The Barony of Glasgow was one of these, being the bishop's territory in the immediate vicinity of the cathedral. North of the Clyde, this domain extended from Partick in the west to Carmyle in the east. The eastern boundary was where it met the property of the Newbattle monks, hence the name of modern Monklands district. The bishop's country seat was at Bishop Loch, and legend has it that he was even able to sail there from his palace at a time when the east end lochs were larger and linked.

With its growth in prestige and power, the cathedral at Glasgow required many dignitaries to carry out particular offices, and from his estates the bishop had to provide each with land from which they could derive an income. Some of these allocations were known as prebends and could be very extensive; the prebend of Barlanark, for example, covered about 2,000 acres. In addition to the clerics, the bishop also had to make provision for the burgh of Glasgow, which was established within the Barony around AD 1175-78. Apart from the land required for building, the inhabitants were allocated plots where they could grow their own food. Common land was set aside to the west and east of the burgh where they could graze their livestock and gather fuel for their fires.

The enormous wealth of the Church attracted the attention of the powerful and greedy, and the corruption which ensued directly contributed to its deposition at the Reformation in 1560. The territory of the Barony was divided, with fragments coming into the possession of many different owners. It is from amongst the early renters of Church land and the merchants of the fledgling burgh that some of the more notable east-end families arose. With the demise of the Church many had managed to obtain title to its land through various means, and held onto it for centuries afterwards. The great Barlanark estate passed to the Baillie family through the exploitation of their position of power within the Church. Other families who had originally rented Church land were the Bogles of Shettleston, Daldowie and Carmyle, the Grays of Tollcross, Dalmarnock and Carntyne and the Waddrops, also of Dalmarnock and Dalbeth.

The common land of the burgh was eventually sold off by the town fathers – mostly to themselves – in the seventeenth century to cover debts. To the east, this gave rise to the large Barrowfield estate upon which Calton and Bridgeton were later built. For several centuries the memory of the lordship was preserved with the establishment of the Barony Parish in around 1599 by the Reformed Church, but this too was eventually consigned to the history books. However, the burgh to which the Barony gave rise thrived to a degree undreamt of and, with the passage of years and the city's expansion, the old lordship was finally brought within Glasgow's boundary along with some of the Newbattle land.

Scotland was not greatly endowed with fertile ground, and the bishop's holdings were no exception to the generality: much of the territory to the east was waterlogged moss, lochs, moorland and forest. The little that could be cultivated was usually rented out. Over time, small separate hamlets developed in association with farming. Later, these and other hamlets grew with the advent of weaving as an important occupation, and through the mining industry. The late eighteenth century saw the larger-scale enclosure and improvement of land into country estates, but these were relatively short-lived. The progress of the Industrial Revolution saw the creation of new villages whose own boundaries expanded until many communities coalesced into the districts known today, such as Parkhead and Baillieston.

Glasgow's own growth eastwards was driven by the need to accommodate a hugely increased population, commercial and industrial base. Gradually, the old and new villages were swallowed up by their very large neighbour. In 1846 the Burgh of Calton, along with Mile-end, Bridgeton, Dalmarnock, Dennistoun, Camlachie and part of Parkhead were added. Then followed Shettleston and Tollcross (1912), Millerston and Carntyne (1926), Hogganfield and east Carntyne (1931), Gartloch, Easterhouse and Queenslie (1938), and Mount Vernon and Baillieston (1975). The acquisition of land for housing in particular was a powerful force which in the twentieth century resulted in housing schemes across Carntyne, Ruchazie, Cranhill, Garthamlock and, most notably, Easterhouse. The cost was the loss of many of the rural aspects of the terrain, with farms replaced by crops of houses. Much of the inter-war housing stock was of good quality and has stood the test of time, requiring only repairs and renovation. The post-Second World War Corporation estates, where quality was necessarily sacrificed to quantity, have not faired nearly so well. After just fifty years, most of this housing stock has now been replaced with new houses.

Some of the most significant changes in the east end in recent decades resulted from the Glasgow Eastern Area Renewal (GEAR) project. Initiated in 1976, GEAR was an attempt to address the economic decline and deprivation of 4,000 acres of this part of the city, to stimulate the economy, tackle social problems and create a more attractive environment. Large areas of Calton, Bridgeton and Dalmarnock were demolished in the process, to the extent that by 1981 the population of the GEAR area was reduced from 82,000 to just over 38,000. Economic resurrection was not achieved, but there were certainly major changes, leaving the old areas barely recognisable.

In this collection of images I have tried to find photographs which are less well known to the devotees of east Glasgow history, and seldom, if ever, published before. There is a wealth of material available from postcards of the Edwardian period, but I have also used photographs from more recent times, taken within living memory, and especially prior to the major changes to the inner-city areas. I sincerely hope you enjoy them and that they remind you of happy days.

On occasion I have used the definite article 'the' in front of Calton, London Road, Gallowgate, etc, as this is how some streets and other locations are often spoken of locally. Also, use of the term 'east end' is considered by some (myself included) to refer only to the older, inner city areas such as Calton, Bridgeton Dennistoun and Parkhead. Hence my adoption of the expression east Glasgow in referring to other places, as this encompasses the entire city as far as its eastern boundary.

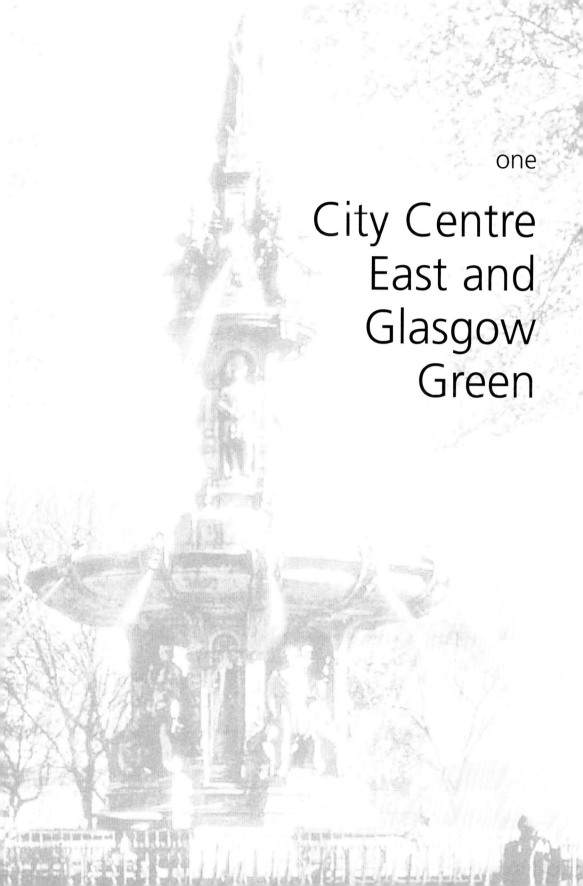

one

City Centre East and Glasgow Green

Above: Glasgow Cathedral from the north at the turn of nineteenth century, depicting a rural aspect that has long since passed; the Molendinar Burn flows open to the sky as it did when St Ninian consecrated a burial place on its western bank late in the fourth century. This was overshadowed by the arrival of St Mungo almost a century later. The site and the church which rose upon St Mungo's burial place became the heart around which Glasgow grew.

Below: Glasgow's second most prestigious medieval building, the Bishop's Castle, is sketched here in around 1792, just before its removal to make room for the Royal Infirmary. First documented in 1258, the castle was the temporal power base of Glasgow's spiritual lords. It was occupied by the English during the War of Independence, and later by the French in support of Queen Mary. Some remnants of the foundations can still be seen in the vicinity of St Mungo's Museum, which was built on its site.

From the cathedral, the Bridge of Sighs spans a now culverted Molendinar Burn, providing the main entrance to the Necropolis. During the early Victorian era, traditional churchyards could no longer meet the demand for burial. This led to the development of commercial burial grounds. Laid out on the Fir Park, Glasgow's new 'City of the Dead' opened in 1833 and by the turn of the twentieth century had provided a last resting place for many of the city's great and good. Dominating the vista, with his column on the summit of the hill, is the 1825 memorial statue of John Knox.

From 1799 to 1889 the Barony church of Scotland was situated to the south of the cathedral – 'the ugliest Kirk in all Europe' according to one of its ministers, Dr Norman McLeod. The church took its name from the ancient feudal patrimony of the Bishops and Archbishops of Glasgow; the Barony of Glasgow. The parish was established in around 1595 and for just over 200 years the congregation had met in the crypt of the cathedral; it even featured in Sir Walter Scott's *Rob Roy*. The new building was designed by James Adam and, like most buildings set in proximity to the cathedral, it created controversy over its appearance. It is seen here probably during its final years.

The Royal Infirmary, 'the Royal', was opened in 1794 as a voluntary hospital in close association with the university and for more than a century the Robert Adam building (built in around 1910) faced into what is now Cathedral Precinct. For a period from the 1890s, part of Castle Street beside the hospital was actually paved with wood to present the noise from traffic disturbing the patients. The Adam building was replaced in 1914 by the present building, which has been criticised for overwhelming the cathedral. The infirmary has traditionally provided a service to the eastern districts, and is highly valued by the inhabitants. The complex of buildings now extends along Castle Street into Alexandra Parade.

The Royal Asylum for the Blind provided accommodation for poor children and aged women, as well as a variety of educational, training and employment opportunities to other blind persons. It was located in Castle Street from 1829 to 1935. The remnants of one of its buildings, complete with spire and clock tower, now sits wedged between old and new parts of the Royal Infirmary. The hospital acquired it from the asylum and used it until 1989. A dominant feature, seen here in around 1904, is the statue reflecting the Victorian religious-based philanthropy of the age. It represents Christ in medieval garb, restoring sight to a blind child.

Ladywell is one of the city's oldest streets, although the part shown here at the junction with Duke Street is now submerged beneath the Wellpark Brewery. The street wound up to the cathedral and probably came into existence as a route to a nearby well – the Lady Well of its name. This building, seen here in around 1902, was believed to be the last thatched house in Glasgow.

The site of the Lady Well is marked by an elaborate urn set within a niche in the graveyard wall. Springs and wells were always a very important source of clean water and were used in Glasgow even after the city introduced supplies from Loch Katrine in the mid-nineteenth century. It is thought that the Lady Well was only abandoned due to its proximity to the new graveyard, and fears of contamination.

Above: Scrubbing casks clean at the Tennent Wellpark Brewery, 1910. Hugh and Robert Tennent opened their premises at Drygate Bridge in 1740, but the family had been associated with brewing in Glasgow since around 1556. Now part of Tennent Caledonian Breweries, Tennent's notable advertising campaigns have included the introduction of the 'Lager Lovelies' cans and sponsorship of the 'T in the Park' music festival.

Below: The acquisition of a brand-new truck probably prompted this display of 'transport through the ages' in the main avenue, previously St Anne's Street, through Tennent's Wellpark Brewery, *c.* 1935. The company's highly recognisable 'T' trademark is prominent to the right.

Alexandra Parade at the 'Tobacco Land' west end. This area derived its nickname from the tobacco factories and warehouses situated there. A large, almost Art-Deco building was constructed from 1946-53 for W.D. & H.O. Wills, whose cigarette brands included Woodbine, Capstan and Embassy. It was photographed in 2002, eight years after cigarette production had ceased. The building's fortunes revived with an award-winning conversion into City Park, which lets office space to a variety of enterprises.

In Duke Street, at the bottom of John Knox Street, the old Great Eastern Hotel sits facing an uncertain future. Built as a mill in 1849, it was converted into a private hotel for 450 working men in 1907. Initially offering a higher standard of accommodation than the city's 'model lodging houses', in its latter years it declined into notoriety. It became the repository for society's unfortunate, neglected and abandoned. It was acquired by the Loretto Housing Association in 1994 which decanted its remaining residents to the Association's newly developed accommodation in the old Duke Street Hospital. It finally closed its doors in 2000, missed by few.

Overshadowed by Duke Street Prison, a Coronation tram makes its way eastwards along Duke Street, 1959. The old country road, Carntyne Lone, was replaced by Duke Street in 1794. One suggestion for its new name was its proximity to the Duke of Montrose's old town residence in Drygate. Another is that it was named for the Duke of York. Whichever was the case, it gained a reputation as the longest street in the kingdom.

Duke Street Prison, 1955. The prison was built from 1792 and gradually extended uphill towards Drygate. It was ever a dismal presence, and was not missed by its neighbours when demolished in around 1960, its role having been taken over by Barlinnie. Most frequently recalled as a place of execution to the accompaniment of an unfurled black flag and tolling prison bell, its less notorious inmates included the notable socialist John McLean and the militant suffragette Dr Elizabeth Chalmers Smith. Children borne within the prison were compensated with a lifetime allowance of a farthing a day.

Glasgow's first university, or college as it was also known in its earlier days, was established in 1451 by a Papal Bull. Using a house named the 'Auld Pedagogy' in Rottenrow as an initial base, it moved to a rented tenement on the east side of High Street within two years. This proved to be the nucleus around which the college grew and the site it was to occupy for over 400 years. From the mid-seventeenth century onwards a beautiful complex of buildings were constructed to accommodate its expansion. The site eventually extended to encompass twenty-six acres, which included gardens leading down to the Molendinar Burn and the first Hunterian Museum. The gatehouse on High Street is shown here in around 1870. Although usually on good terms, there was occasional friction between the scholars and townspeople – 'town and gown' disputes. When the resurrectionists became active in the early nineteenth century, the college staff were believed to be complicit in their body-snatching activities and it was attacked on no less that four occasions. Sadly, the locality degenerated over time and the college became hemmed in by slums, the attendant squalor making it a very unhealthy place to live. Like others who could afford to do so, a move westwards was agreed. The site was sold to the Glasgow Union Railway in 1863 and a new home was built at Gilmorehill by 1870. Although some parts of the old college were saved, such as the lion and unicorn staircase and those elements now incorporated into the Pearce Lodge, the demolition of the rest was a huge loss to the architectural heritage of the city.

Above: The Mercat Building at Glasgow Cross sits between the streams of traffic moving along the medieval Gallowgate and the more recent 1824 London Road. To the building's rear, a steam train crosses the bridge built by the City of Glasgow Union Railway which transects these routes. The building was constructed from 1925-28 and, despite a seventeenth-century appearance, the Mercat Cross in front was built in 1929.

Below: Watson Street, off the Gallowgate, is now rather nondescript, but in 1884, fourteen people died in the Star Variety Theatre following panic caused when a false fire alarm was raised. On 19 November, 1905 it became the setting for a real fire in which thirty-nine men were killed in the model lodging house at the Gallowgate junction.

Above: Glasgow recognised the need for a fire service as early as 1656 with its purchase of a fire engine following two devastating 'great fires' which destroyed significant parts of the city. By the time of the Watson Street fire it was in a much better position to tackle such blazes, but larger firms still found it worth making their own arrangements, such as the Wellpark Brewery brigade of 1905. Glasgow went on to develop an unenviable reputation as the 'tinderbox' city as its Victorian housing stock became increasingly dilapidated.

Below: Despite its significant role in the history of Glasgow, this rare view of the Molendinar Burn near Duke Street at about the end of the nineteenth century shows just how polluted it was allowed to become. No longer fit for drinking water or suitable as a power source, it degenerated into a sewer. The burn was diverted into culverts for much of its length within the city and was seldom seen until it reached the Clyde.

Another medieval Glasgow street of which no trace remains other than the route itself is the Saltmarket. Running towards the Clyde from Glasgow Cross, its name was changed from the Waulkergate in 1650 when the actual salt market moved there. The Lord Protector, Oliver Cromwell, resided in the Saltmarket when he invaded Scotland in 1650, unhappy at its support for Charles II. Traffic was apparently less hectic in 1907, and folk seemed to feel safe enough to stand in the road itself.

An 18A tram on London Road at Charlotte Street in 1959 approaches the sharp bend to the north east which has become a part of local legend. When London Street was opened up from the Saltmarket it was intended that it take a direct route along Monteith Row to Barrowfield Toll (now Bridgeton Cross) to provide an alternative route to the highly congested Gallowgate. The row's highly influential residents are believed to have ensured the change of direction which diverted the road through Balaam's Pass instead and into what was then Great Hamilton Street, behind the row, thus securing its seclusion and view of the Green.

Above: The Clyde forms the southern boundary of Glasgow Green and for centuries has served as a water source and a transport route. It has provided salmon for food and, in some places, even gold and fresh-water pearls. Seen here in 1837, the Green seems to have been a pleasant place for a stroll, with the river providing the opportunity for boating. Swimming was not advisable due to pollution. This view is from where King's Drive now intersects the Green, separating off Provost's Haugh. The seat circling the tree traditionally marked the spot where Bonnie Prince Charlie reviewed his army on the Haugh in 1745.

Below: Where the town meets the Green: Glasgow's Green was located downriver from the Saltmarket, but through the centuries it was lost to development as the new Green to the east was enlarged. This sketch of 1825 depicts the fair at the Saltmarket. Glasgow's right to hold an annual fair dates back to the twelfth century. Once held near the cathedral, it eventually moved down to the river.

The Green provides a historical setting for a range of buildings, monuments and statues. Its own version of the 'Arc de Triomphe' even adorns the new Saltmarket entrance. The McLennan Arch is the oldest artefact on the Green and was part of the façade of Robert and James Adam's 1796 Glasgow Assembly Rooms (the Athenaeum). When the Assembly Rooms were taken down in 1892, it was saved by Baillie James McLennan and presented to the city, and given his name in commemoration.

On Monday 9 May 2005, a fully restored and functioning Doulton Fountain was unveiled by the Lord Provost at a new location in front of the People's Palace Museum. This remarkable terracotta structure is reputedly the largest of its kind in the world and was produced by Doulton & Co. for the Glasgow Exhibition of 1888 at Kelvingrove Park. The fountain's theme is a celebration of the British Empire, then at the peak of its power, surmounted by a statue of the Queen-Empress Victoria. It was gifted to the city following the exhibition and relocated to Glasgow Green in 1890; it is shown here in 1955. What was once one of the saddest sights on Glasgow Green due to vandalism is now one of the most spectacular.

Built on the Green from 1895-98, the People's Palace incorporated a museum, art galleries and Winter Gardens with a music-hall facility. The museum was to form permanent collections to serve as a repository for the preservation of the history of the city and its industry, and the galleries were to enrich the cultural life of the east end. This made it quite unique for the time. The Palace has managed to survive fire and potential demolition, and has entered into the affections of east-enders as fully as the Green itself.

The sculpture seen here, displayed for a few years in the Winter Gardens, was the plaster model for 'St Mungo as the Patron of Art and Music' of 1900 which now sits at the north entrance to Kelvingrove. The Winter Gardens were intended to provide a green and warm haven in the depths of a Glasgow winter (and some summers), but it was the heat and humidity that eventually destroyed the plaster model. The Gardens provide an enjoyable setting for musical events, wedding celebrations or even just a cup of tea and a scone.

The museum has acquired a very wide range of memorabilia and curios relating to the city's history over the years – from the socialist John McLean's desk to props from Billy Connolly's stage act. Many items are incorporated into tableaux which provide a glimpse into the past, adding a depth of meaning and sense of history which can be lost in more traditional displays. These very popular presentations have included reconstructions of a chemist's shop, a dairy, a Victorian bathroom, and a cubicle from Clyde Street Home. The 'single end' or single-room house shown here was a very popular exhibit in the 1970s.

Not everyone came to the Green to relax; generations of Glasgow women used the Green to do their washing in the water from the river and burns. The clothes would then be spread out to bleach and dry. Castle Boins was one area on the banks of the Camlachie Burn which was particularly popular. The unusual name was derived from the hundreds of tubs, or boynes, to be found there in which the women tread their washing. This tradition has endured. The children seen here in around 1900 are still treading their washing almost in the shadow of Greenhead Wash House.

The area of the Green at King's Drive was added in 1773. It was here during Victoria's reign that an open-air gymnasium and a children's playground were created. The last is seen here in around 1900 with a rather sedate and well-dressed group of children, perhaps from the more well-to-do part of Bridgeton at Greenhead Street. Unlike many of the modern materials used in the new adventure playground which has replaced the old facilities, the cast iron and tarmac of the recreational areas were rather unforgiving when accidents occurred.

There are now five river crossings (and a weir) from the Green to the southern bank. Until St Andrew's suspension bridge opened in 1855, workers crossing to and from Hutchesontown on the opposite bank had to use a ferry service. The bridge replaced this and cost 2d per week to use. Local children called it the 'shaky bridge' because of the vibration they thought they detected when jumping up and down on it! This 1975 photo also shows the United Co-operative Baking Society's building in the background.

Above: Calton and Bridgeton encroach upon the northern boundaries of the Green and with the park being quite flat many nearby buildings are readily visible on its fringes from a distance. In this view of around 1905 (to the left of the bandstand) is the splendidly ornate façade of Templeton's carpet factory. To the right is the 1878 Greenhead Baths & Wash House with its clock tower. Greenhead was the first Glasgow 'steamie.'

Below: R. & J. Dick's Gutta Percha Works, about the same date, was famous for its production of gutta percha and balata goods. These materials are a natural product related to rubber. When moulded into shoes, the former of these gave rise to the Glaswegian name for sandshoes – gutties.

It is mainly for football that the Provost's Haugh is now known. Acquired by the city in 1792, the area had been very low lying and prone to regular flooding – however, the ground level was raised about 100 years ago and the football pitches seen here were laid out on the flattened top. Before being largely converted to grass and synthetic surfaces for the new football centre, this image of footballers in 1955 raising the dust of the red gravel pitches was very familiar, except when they had been transformed into a mud bath by the rain! At least one of the players seen here seems to have acquired the almost obligatory gravel graze.

For a brief period at the height of the summer, the carnival came to the pitches, and provided a distraction for adults and children alike in the weeks leading up to their fair fortnight holidays. At one time the shows included attractions such as a circus and a boxing booth, but these increasingly gave way to mechanised entertainments like the 'Rib Tickler', 'Ghost Train' or 'Dive Bombers'. A Chairoplane in full flight is seen here in 1955. The shows had migrated to the pitches following its period of exile to Vinegarhill in Camlachie in 1870 from the western end of the Green, but have now moved to an area near Nelson's Monument.

Left: East Glasgow has a strong association with James Watt (1736-1819). He worked at Glasgow University as a mathematical instrument maker from 1757-63. As a civil engineer he surveyed the route of the Monkland Canal, and is reputed to have designed the first Rutherglen Bridge. However, it is as the inventor of the separate condenser for the steam engine that he is renowned worldwide. The idea came to Watt on Glasgow Green and the event is commemorated by a large inscribed stone to the south of Nelson's Monument. Give the repercussions of his invention, the scale of the memorial seems rather constrained. Even the statue, which once stood on the Dassy Green before being removed to the more protective environs of the People's Palace, is second-hand: it was made for the Atlantic Mills in Bridgeton and donated to the Corporation in 1936.

Below: At the Green's eastern-most extremity at Rutherglen Bridge, embedded in a retaining wall, is a tablet commemorating 'The Site of Allan's Pen', just seen here centre picture in 1974. Alexander Allan acquired the Newhall estate in the late eighteenth century and decided to create direct access to the riverside from it. He had a ramp built down to the river, and led the existing path along the banks and through a tunnel beneath it. The path was not blocked, but his action outraged local opinion to the extent that Allan, as an employer, was boycotted. The problem was resolved fairly quickly when the Clyde flooded and swept the construction away.

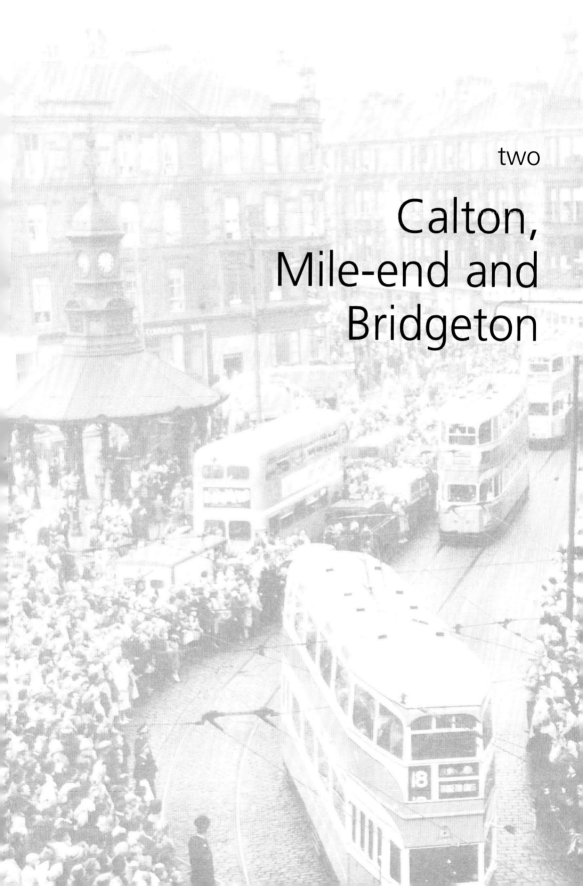

two

Calton,
Mile-end and
Bridgeton

Established in 1705 on the western part of the Barrowfield estate as 'Blackfauld', Calton acquired its current name in around 1723 whilst temporarily owned by Glasgow. Calton had started very slowly, as a community of weavers, but its proximity to Glasgow eventually spurred a fairly rapid development as an industrial suburb. It remained independent of Glasgow until 1846. Stevenson Street, seen above in around 1916, was formerly Calton's High Street before taking the name of the Burgh's second provost, Nathaniel Stevenson. This was how the early Calton looked, but all of these eighteenth and early nineteenth-century buildings were swept away in the slum clearances of the post-First World War period. Only two eighteenth-century buildings have been preserved, on the Gallowgate.

A coal ree (yard) in Thomson's Lane with pantiled roof, c. 1916. Calton was probably one of the earliest products of the Industrial Revolution. It is thought that coal was dug at Calton from a very early time – hence the original name of 'Blackfauld' or black field. Certainly local clay deposits were exploited for centuries. This clay was used to produce bricks and pantiles as well as other goods from the new community's potteries: these provided a readily available source of building material for the construction of the one- and two-storey houses and workshops which came to dominate the area. Glasgow was also able to avail itself of these local materials during a period of very rapid growth.

Memorial and dedication service, 27 May 1931. Calton Burying Ground in Abercromby Street was opened for use in May 1787, and within a matter of months, three of those weavers killed by the military at the bloody conclusion to the Weavers' Strike of 1787 were buried there. More than 6,000 people attended the funeral; equivalent to almost half the population of the Calton at the time. The strike having proven an extreme hardship, no stone was placed over the graves until 1836, when a memorial was paid for by public subscription. It was renovated in 1931 and 1957, and an additional stone provided by the Glasgow Trades Council in 1931.

The Barras at London Road, c. 1916. Prior to the First World War, Maggie McIver and her husband built, repaired and hired out barrows to hawkers in the Calton. They then acquired vacant sites to build stalls and gradually established a permanent market, which was enclosed and roofed over in 1928. The Barras fulfilled a much-needed function in the less well-off east end. Bargains of all sorts, from second-hand clothing to household goods, a cycle or even an anchor, could be acquired for next to nothing.

Early eighteenth-century Glasgow was an expanding, but still beautiful, city which required an inn worthy of it. Robert Tennent was allowed to purchase the site of the derelict Little St Mungo's Kirkyard on the Gallowgate by the town council and built the Saracen Head Inn. It opened in 1755, but after only thirty-seven years it was converted into shops and houses. These were taken down in around 1906, just after this photograph was taken, to make way for the tenement which now incorporates the Saracen Head public house.

Eastwards of the bend in London Road sits the 'Old Barns' pub at the junction with Ross Street. The pub pre-dates an earlier, pantile-roofed inn known as the 'Old Burnt Barns', seen here in around 1900. It was supposedly established in 1679, taking its name from a group of thatched houses at the Gallowgate, but the origin of the name itself is lost. Note the cast-iron public drinking fountain that used to be common around Glasgow streets.

Market Day, Graham Square, Gallowgate.

Graham Square, seen here in around 1910, was a failed housing venture masterminded by James Graham, owner of the Saracen Head Inn, in 1783. Its fortunes were not revived until the town council relocated the cattle and horse market to the site in 1818. The Square also provided a setting for feeing days, when farmers and potential workers would come together to negotiate employment and wages for the coming year. In 1927 it was the scene of a tragic blaze in which four fire-fighters lost their lives.

The meat market moved to the same location in 1875; the main passageway is shown here prior to the First World War. Many folk had anecdotes of animals escaping up tenement closes while being driven along the mains roads to the market, which is now defunct. The impressive entrances from Graham Square have been saved, and earlier associations are recalled in features of the Square such as Kenny Hunter's 'Golden Calf' sculpture.

Two main access routes into the Calton from the Gallowgate were Calton Entry and Calton Mouth. This photograph shows Calton Mouth in 1974: its name probably derives from the gaping entranceway. Bain Street stretches into the distance, driven through Calton's slums, and was named after Glasgow's Lord Provost of 1874.

Barrowland, Gallowgate, 1975. The McIvers diversified into the entertainment industry and built the Barrowland Dance Hall over an indoor market. It opened on Christmas Eve 1934, and such was its eventual fame that it was even mentioned in the wartime broadcasts of Lord Haw Haw (the traitor William Joyce, who was hanged after the Second World War). Barrowland burned down in August 1958, but was rebuilt and opened again on Christmas Eve 1960. It no longer operates as a dance hall, but with the closure of the Glasgow Apollo it became the UK venue that major bands such as the Rolling Stones and REM most wanted to play.

Gallowgate looking westwards from its junction with Market Street, 1974. The Gallowgate runs from Glasgow Cross to Burgher Street at Parkhead Cross – a distance of approximately 3,000 metres. However, the original Gallowgate only extended to the present day Great Dovehill Street, where the route was blocked by the town gate known as the East Port. Outside was the rough country road to the village of Camlachie.

London Road looking eastwards from near its junction with Bain Street, 1974. Before being upgraded as part of the town council's improvements to the Green in the early nineteenth century, this was a country road known as Craignestock Lone. To the east, there were no buildings, but Calton Green bordered onto Glasgow Green. Following the building of Monteith Row, the road was renamed Great Hamilton Street. In its final days as a commercial area, this part of London Road was particularly attractive to the motorbiking fraternity, having a greater than usual number of motorbike shops.

The Eastern District police station in Tobago Street, 1974; this 1868 building has been disused for many years now and is falling into dereliction, its function having been taken over by a new station on London Road. While independent, Calton was responsible for policing its own residents. Police authority ended at the Burgh limits, this being the Camlachie Burn in the case of Bridgeton. It seems to have been a popular pastime for Brigtonians to commit an offence in Calton and jump the burn to avoid the consequences!

Tureen Street Public School, built in 1874, in 1974. The street was the setting for an anti-Catholic riot in 1779 when the pottery of a Frenchman, Mr Bagniolle, was attacked. The street name is probably a corruption of Touraine, where Mr Bagniolle came from, instead of being related to his production of tureens as is generally suggested.

St Luke's and St Andrew's Church of Scotland faces across Bain Square towards the Barras, 1975. One of the earliest remaining church buildings in the east end, it was built in 1836-37 as St Luke's to serve western Calton. Its once large parish shrunk as additional churches were built to serve a growing population, only to expand again as it absorbed most of them when this trend reversed – it now combines ten congregations.

St Mary's in Abercromby Street, in 1975. It was only the second Catholic church to have been built in the Glasgow area since the Reformation of 1560, and was sited in Calton in 1842 to meet the needs of a very extensive parish to the east of Glasgow. Finance for the construction was raised in Ireland through the efforts of Father Peter Forbes – with Forbes Street named in his memory. Anecdotal evidence suggests that Pope Pius XII spent some time in the parish during the earlier years of his church career.

Mile-end sprang up along the banks of the Camlachie Burn, to the east of Calton and north of Bridgeton, only falling under the legal jurisdiction of Calton in 1819. The name's origin is not known, but it may be significant that its main street – Broad Street – is almost exactly a mile from Glasgow Cross, the cathedral and Dalmarnock Ford, highly significant places in older times. This back court at Rogart Street in 1933 gives some idea of what the hamlet was like in the early nineteenth century.

The fields around Broad Street were soon occupied by a variety of industries, including weaving mills and heavy engineering works. Mavor & Coulson Ltd opened their Broad Street electrical engineering factory in 1897, and wired the world's largest woollen mill near St Petersburg! Later, it became a major innovator in the production of mine-working equipment – one of its workshops is shown here. As Anderson Tunnelling it closed in the mid-1990s as a result of the virtual elimination of the British mining industry.

Opposite above: Christ Church in Crownpoint Road was established in 1835. It was one of the first churches to be built by the Scottish Episcopal Church after its reconciliation with the Government following its earlier commitment to the Jacobite cause of the Catholic Stuarts. The church drew a local congregation but for forty years it also served the soldiers of the Gallowgate Barracks who would march there on Sundays. The officers favoured the more exclusive St Andrew's-by-the-Green. The last service was held on the 18 June 1978.

Opposite below: David Dale College, Broad Street, 1974. The college was opened in 1949 to help meet the increased demand for further education after the Second World War. It was named after the eighteenth-century philanthropist in recognition of his efforts to advance the education of his young workers. Partly due of the decline in the locals industries which supplied a significant part of its student intake, it closed in 1974. The pipework seen traversing the street indicates the proximity of the John Lyle & Co., a carpet-weaving rival to Templeton's.

When the City Improvement Trust undertook slum clearance at Barrowfield Toll in the early 1870s, the new Cross was formed. The centre piece was the 50ft high cast-iron pavilion by the Sun Foundry which was erected in 1875. It was called 'the Umbrella' locally because of the shelter it provided against the elements.

Building Rutherglen Bridge was a joint undertaking by Rutherglen and Glasgow to facilitate trade. It was opened in 1776 and linked the Barrowfield lands on the northern bank of the Clyde to Shawfield on the southern – giving rise to the village of Bridgetown, later known as Bridgeton (or Brigton to the local people). Its demolition in 1891 is shown here.

Unlike most Glasgow villages, Bridgeton retained its Main Street, which runs between Rutherglen Bridge and Bridgeton Cross. Bridgeton developed along this street but few of the earlier buildings seen here in 1974 remain. The structure with the ornate façade was the headquarters for the 7th (The Blythswood) Battalion of the HLI.

Bridgeton Cross became an exceptionally busy intersection for several major roads leading into the city before the advent of the M8 motorway. One of these was Dalmarnock Road, seen here in 1974 from opposite Dunn Street towards the Cross with a glimpse of the Ruby Street high flats in the background.

London Road, Glasgow (No. 1)

Everything is this view of London Road looking eastwards in around 1909 has gone. The main landmark seen here is the London Road church at Brook Street, so named because of its proximity to the Camlachie Burn. There was such an outcry over the state of this main artery into the city in the 1970s that it was intensively landscaped.

The only high flats in Bridgeton are at Ruby Street, built in the 1960s. This view is from Baltic Street at Fairbairn Street looking westwards in 1974. The tenements are on their 'last legs' after almost sixty years, but the new flats had already lost their appeal as the housing of the future and no more were built.

Bridgeton Cross, Glasgow   PN5215

The Olympia, seen here in around 1960, has dominated the northern side of Bridgeton Cross since it opened in 1911 as a Theatre of Varieties. It made a very successful transition to picture hall in 1923 and was the more up-market of the local houses. When it finally closed in 1974 it was the only cinema left in the district.

In 1910 a skating rink in James Street was converted into the King's Picture Theatre. Competition soon arose from the 'wee' Royal in Main Street the following year: the Royal was cheap and popular, routinely including sweets, fruit or a comic for children in the admission price. The same children could surreptitiously move from the wooden benches to the more comfortable, and expensive, cushioned seats under cover of darkness. In the end the King's managed to outlast the Royal by one year when it closed down in 1959. It is seen here is 1975 as a furniture showroom. The Art-Deco façade was added in 1936.

A chimney sweep such as James McGill – seen here in James Street in 1915 – was a common sight in the days when all households depended on coal fires for cooking and heating. Unswept 'lums' could catch fire – which could spread to the rest of a building – so the sweep provided an essential service; it was considered lucky to meet a sweep, particularly on your wedding day. With the introduction of legislation to reduce air pollution, coal fires were mostly relegated to history within the city, along with the sweep's profession.

A back court at No. 37 Dale Street in 1920. As piped water was gradually introduced to tenements, many even had their own wash houses round the 'back'. In the early morning, the boiler would be lit and the water boiled, possibly with a Dolly Blue to clean the whites first of all. Then the coloureds would follow. The 'boilins' might be offered to a succession of neighbours. It many respects it was a very social event. Co-operative efforts might be needed with larger items for mangling, and the opportunity taken to chat while working or during breaks. People would take agreed turns at the wash house as well as the back for drying. Allocated days were jealously guarded.

Into the 1970s it was seldom necessary to leave most inner-city districts to find whatever you needed in the shops. Shopping was a very social activity, it being almost impossible to walk up and down Main Street without meeting someone you knew. This newsagent and tobacconists was possibly sited in John Street in the early 1900s. Mitchells and F & J Smith were both Glasgow-based tobacco merchants.

The Highland Light Infantry have a strong association with Bridgeton. A group are seen here bidding farewell to their loved ones at Bridgeton Station in 1914. Those who did not return from the First World War are commemorated by a Celtic cross on the Dassy Green.

Once the intervening buildings were taken down in the 1970s, the 1836 Bridgeton Parish church faced directly across Dale Street to the Sacred Heart Chapel. As with Glasgow generally, conflict existed for generations between the Protestant and Catholic communities of Bridgeton. Norman Street gave its name to the Catholic gang, the 'Norman Conks', while the most notorious of gangs, the Protestant 'Brigton Billy Boys', was named after its founder member, William Fullerton. The Bridgeton church closed in 1985.

The Sacred Heart mission in Old Dalmarnock Road, seen here in 1974, was opened in 1873. The original wooden building was replaced in 1909-10 by the present imposing red sandstone edifice in the form of a Roman basilica. The highly ornate interior contains an interesting curio – mounted on the pulpit is a metal crucifix which was found by a local man during the First World War while he was digging a trench. He was later hit by enemy fire, but the bullet was deflected by the crucifix, which he had kept in his tunic.

The earliest educational facilities were inevitably associated with the Church, and this tradition continued after the Reformation. Bridgeton Free church established a school in Hozier Street in 1849 which was later absorbed into the national system. It became John Street Primary, seen here in 1974 shortly before closure. The school was a 'feeder' to John Street Secondary in Tullis Street.

John Street Primary School photo, c. 1964. Those identified include Jim Hosey, Jim Donnelly, James Corbally (?), Billy Walker, David Brady, Daniel Ferguson, Charlie Forrest, Gordon Hutcheson, Gordon Adams, Alex Connelly, Walter Keen, Rita Martin, Elizabeth Montgumery, Jean Woods, Freddie Bell, Sandra Crawford, Senga Findlay, Mary Martin, Ruby Edgar, Rita Drummond (?), Helen Dickson, Isobel McTavish, Linda McCool (?), Alan Short, Alex McGarvey and Frank McLaren.

The original Bridgeton Cross is recorded as having been at the junction of Dale Street and Reid Street, but it seems never to have been marked by anything more than a few stones in the road, and even those have disappeared. The present Cross is still referred to as the 'Toll' as it was formed at Barrowfield Toll. The Camlachie Burn used to flow through this area and marked the boundary between Bridgeton and Calton; a bridge crossed the burn, and this was where toll charges were collected. As part of 1870 improvements, the burn was culverted and the northern section of the Toll widened. The blond sandstone buildings provided through the City Improvement Trust around the Cross were later supplemented by the red sandstone Bridgeton Central station and tenements (1892), Bridgeton Cross Mansions (1899), Glasgow Savings Bank (1902), the Olympia Theatre (1911) and the Salvation Army citadel (1927). The Toll was probably a popular meeting place from its earliest days. It still provides a focus for a variety of gatherings and processions, but it is unlikely that it has seen anything as spectacular as the last tram procession on 2 September 1962, shown here. Fortunately, Bridgeton Cross was classed as one of the 'core areas' to be preserved during the GEAR (Glasgow Eastern Area Renewal) decade and, apart from the 'missing' south-western corner, this was accomplished.

three

Dennistoun, Camlachie and Parkhead

Alexandra Park was laid out by the City Improvement Trust from 1866–70 on the lands of Wester Kennyhill and extended a few years later with the addition of Easter Kennyhill. It was named after Alexandra, Princess of Wales. Alexandra Parade (seen here looking eastwards from Meadowpark Street in around 1908), or 'the Parade', as it is often abbreviated to, provided a link to the new park from Townhead.

The rapid growth in cycling as a recreation that took place in Edwardian times is represented in this image of Alexandra Parade, c. 1907. It was a liberating innovation for women in particular. Perhaps the cyclist seen here intends cycling around Alexandra Park, the gates of which she is approaching. Her destination may even be St Andrew's United Free church in the distance, now St Andrew's East Church of Scotland.

Music in the parks became such an attraction that the original cast-iron bandstands gave way to larger auditoria. As seen here in around 1930, these could draw large crowds, although inevitably the kindness of the weather was a factor. What could have been more pleasant on a summer's evening than meeting friends and enjoying the entertainment?

A gardener's job is never done during the height of summer, and it continues amidst those people lucky enough to have the time to sit and enjoy the fruits of his labours. The engineers seem seldom far away from Glasgow's fountains, and keeping them working seems to present a continual challenge. The superb cast-iron MacFarlane Fountain in Alexandra Park provides a contrast with the Green's terracotta Doulton Fountain. Built at the Walter MacFarlane & Co.'s Saracen Foundry for the 1901 International Exhibition at Kelvingrove, it was moved to the park in around 1910.

Children's fascination with water was well catered for in Alexandra Park, from a look at the ornamental pond and fountain to actually taking to it in your boat, as seen here in the 1950s. The northern areas are still given over to golf, mostly on the slopes of the drumlin created by glacial action during the last ice age. Another example of a drumlin is Shettleston Hill in Tollcross Park.

This paddling pool was created on the site of the old iron bandstand, *c.* 1933. These were often called a 'sauny pon' because a border of simulated beach was often included. This created the illusion of the seaside for those who simply could not afford a holiday away. The pond has now been replaced by a children's play area.

A little bit of greenery in the heart of Dennistoun, and one of many still operating in the east end, the Whitevale Bowling Green, now at the top of Whitehill Street, was founded in 1836 in the Whitevale area – hence its name. The scene has changed little since this photograph was taken at the turn of the century.

Although it may look like it, this is not another pond in Alexandra Park – it is the junction of Meadowpark and Roebank Streets in Dennistoun. Parts of the east end have always been susceptible to flooding, especially those closest to the Clyde, but on this occasion some tenants were forced to leave their homes as the water level rose following a torrential downpour on 30 July 2002.

Meadowpark Street, *c.* 1911. This road takes its name from one of the eighteenth-century estates formed across this part of east Glasgow. The street directly connected Duke Street with Alexandra Parade until the new Whitevale swimming baths blocked the route. The building with the 'floating' staircase to the left was the Dennistoun Wardlaw Congregational church until it closed in 1974, and is now the Christian Fellowship Centre.

Whitehill School at Finlay Drive and Whitehill Street, *c.* 1940. Highly regarded for its academic success, its motto was *Altiora Peto* – 'I Aim Higher.' It was built in 1891 on the former grounds of Whitehill House, the residence of the estate of that name, and at one time it was the property of Alexander Dennistoun.

Above: The boys of Onslow Drive Public School at their woodwork class in 1916. Several of the older Dennistoun schools continue to fulfil their role today, such as Alexandra Parade Primary. Secondary education locally is met by the Whitehill School at Onslow Drive, which opened in 1977.

Below: The young women of Dennistoun Public School in their domestic science class, 1916. These two photographs demonstrate how men and women's roles in society were still very clearly divided. The effects of the First World War, which was being fought at this time, would help change the situation: for example, women over thirty had gained the right to vote by 1918.

The most well-known display in the extensive East End Exhibition buildings at the top of Hillfoot Street was Buffalo Bill Cody's 'Wild West Show' of 1891-92. During its run, Cody became a familiar sight in Duke Street and Gallowgate pubs, while the Native Americans camped at Vinegar Hill, Camlachie, or stayed with local residents. One legacy was the name adopted by a local gang; the Dennistoun Redskins.

As the popularity of the 'flicks' grew, travelling shows and temporary venues such as Corporation halls could no longer cope with the demand. Some music halls or variety theatres were simply converted, but Pringle's Dennistoun Palladium adapted a skating rink at the top of Hillfoot and operated between about 1912-1921. The staff group of that period, shown here, includes what appears to be a string quartet which would have played in accompaniment to the silent films. It was only with the advent of the 'talkies' that this ended.

Continuing a tradition of entertainment which seems to have arisen in the area at the head of Hillfoot Street, the first Dennistoun Palais de Danse was built on the site of the Palladium in 1922. Following a fire, the much-improved hall was reopened in 1938 to compete with its Gallowgate rival, Barrowland. The halls tended to have resident bands. Where Barrowland had the Gaybirds, the Palais had Lauri Blandford and his orchestra. With the decline in the popularity of the dance hall in the 1960s, it was finally converted into a supermarket.

Westercraigs, looking south to the King's Cross junction with Bellgrove Street, *c.* 1930. This was the earliest street of the Dennistoun suburb to be laid out and it contains a variety of detached and semi-detached villas. This had been the design intended for the whole of Dennistoun, but the western part of the suburb was soon given over to tenement construction to meet the demand for houses. The spire belongs to the old Blackfriars church, the congregation of which had moved to this site in 1876 from the High Street. It closed in 1982.

There were times when access to medical aid was largely the province of the rich and powerful. The poor had to depend upon the charity of others, which was often sporadic and meagre. When medical services were finally separated from the poorhouse, Eastern District Hospital was built in 1904. It closed in the mid-1990s, with the main building being converted into flats by the Loretto Housing Association.

The 'heartland' of Alexander Dennistoun's mid-nineteenth-century suburban creation is encompassed within the area created by Alexandra Parade, Duke Street, Westercraigs and Cumbernauld Road. Duke Street to Cumbernauld Road, shown here approximately 100 years ago, remains by far the busiest part.

The other end of Duke Street before it strikes out eastwards towards Parkhead, *c.* 1926. At this point, Cumbernauld Road veers off to the north-east. This is one of the city's many lesser-known crosses, Alexandra Cross; these tended to be Victorian creations intended to lend dignity to the newly-built localities.

Just beyond the junction of Duke Street and Cumbernauld Road is Duke Street station, opened in 1881. In 1959 a steam train emerges from beneath Duke Street *en route* for Springburn via Alexandra Parade – in an era when many a young person dreamed of growing up to be a train driver.

A wedding at St Anne's, Whitehill Street, in August 1990, with the Bluevale flats in the background. St Anne's was built in 1931-33, one of several Catholic churches in the east end designed in association with the celebrated architect Jack Coia: others include St Joachim's, Carmyle; St Maria Goretti, Cranhill; St Paul's, Shettleston and St Benedict's, Easterhouse. Craigpark's Our Lady of Good Counsel is also by Coia.

By the end of the eighteenth century, most of the open land surrounding Glasgow had been enclosed into private estates belonging to the town's gentry. On the ancient Gallowmuir, these included Whitehill, Craigpark, Golfhill and Slatefield, now only recalled in the names of streets formed across them. Mansion houses were built to impress, like Annfield, seen here in about 1870, east of what is now Bellgrove Street.

Above: Bellgrove Street, the northern part of the very old route across the Gallowmuir known as the Common Lone, *c.* 1911. In 1838, John Reid owned the land on either side of the route and upgraded the Lone as part of his plan to develop the whole area. The street was widened, paved and given a new, gentrified name of Bellgrove in keeping with his ambition.

Below: Gallowgate at Bellgrove Street by 1900 was a densely populated main road. It is hard to imagine it as the route through the wild area known as the Gallowmuir, on the great eastern common. The Gallowmuir was bordered by Carntyne Lone (Duke Street) to the north and the lands of Calton and Barrowfield to the south.

Picture houses recognised the need to provide opulent and comfortable surroundings to create the magic of the movies which customers soon came to expect. When one thinks of the term 'picture palace' being applied to the early cinemas, the Orient in the Gallowgate springs to mind. Its entrance, in full Technicolor, looked like a giant wedding cake. It opened in 1932 and could seat 2,570 patrons.

One translation of Camlachie from the Gaelic is 'muddy bend of the burn', which seems apt given that the Camlachie Burn was a major feature of the area. Easter Camlachie, at what is now Janefield Cemetery, was once part of the Tollcross lands. Wester Camlachie extended towards Crownpoint sports complex. The Gallowgate is seen here looking eastwards through Camlachie in 1960 from St Thomas' Gallowgate church.

'Wolfe's House' in Camlachie is mostly remembered for its famous military tenant. In the mid-eighteenth century, Lt-Col (later General) James Wolfe was billeted at Camlachie Mansion. The house had been built in 1720 by John Walkinshaw, who owned both the Camlachie and Barrowfield lands at the time. Wolfe went on to celebrated victories in Quebec during the Canadian wars.

Crown Point is another reminder of Britain's colonial past. Situated at Camlachie Burn, the estate was created by William Alexander and named in commemoration of a British victory over the French in Canada by General Amerhst. Built in 1761, Crown Point house was situated at what is now the junction of Fielden Street and Crownpoint Road. Seen here in the 1960s, it ended its days as office space for the British Basket Works.

Camlachie Primary School, 1964. For most of their recorded history, the Camlachie lands were a focus for mining, with a small hamlet of miners living just south of the Camlachie Lone. Like so much of the area in close proximity to Glasgow, however, Camlachie rapidly became submerged by housing and industrial concerns.

One area, Vinegarhill, was the site of the carnival banished from Glasgow Green in 1870, and supposedly derived its name from the pollution caused by the chemical works there. With growth came community services: Camlachie police station, 1974, on the Gallowgate, was possibly one of the less popular provisions.

Great Eastern Road, later renamed as an extension of the Gallowgate, *c.* 1917. At Parkhead Cross it formed part of the network of roads around which modern Parkhead grew from a collection of separate hamlets of miners and weavers dating from the late eighteenth century. Parkhead's name may derive from the area's proximity to the parkland of the Belvidere estate, where the formation of a village called Helenvale had been considered.

This row of houses at the Duke Street junction with Parkhead Cross extends down Westmuir Street and is typical of early nineteenth-century Parkhead. It is shown here shortly before its demolition in the early 1900s. Westmuir initially had a separate identity from Parkhead, being principally a hamlet of miners' houses.

Above: Parkhead Cross is considered to be one of the best preserved of its kind in Glasgow. The modern Cross is essentially an Edwardian creation to reflect the confidence of a prosperous suburb of the city. The range of highly ornate tenements to the right, seen here shortly after its construction, replaced the buildings shown in the previous photograph. One of the more recent major additions close to the Cross is Parkhead Hospital, which was opened in 1988 in Salamanca Street to replace Gartloch Hospital on the outskirts of the city.

Below: The junction where Westmuir Street and Tollcross Road meet is traditionally known as the 'sheddins', an old Scots word for a place where roads branch. Formerly, this was the site of Parkhead's most familiar landmark, a two-storey building containing Wilson's bakery and facing into the Cross, with a post office on the upper floor. With the closure of Beardmore's Parkhead Forge and the subsequent opening of the Forge shopping complex on its site at Duke Street in 1988, the main focus of commercial activity has moved from the Cross.

Parkhead Forge, originating from a small works of 1837, grew into a huge engineering firm which came to dominate the life of the area, *c.* 1911. In 1794 the entire population of Westmuir and Parkhead was reckoned to be only 678. In 1917, during the First World War, the number of people working at the Forge alone had risen to a massive 27,000, streaming from the works at the end of the day to flood Parkhead.

The engineering works in the east end made a relatively easy transition to the production of armaments during the First World War, with Beardmore's being particularly important to the war effort. This group photograph depicts some of the staff from the howitzer shop, with two gun barrels in view. During the First World War, Beardmore's produced more that 800 of these weapons for the Army.

Westmuir Street, 1999. One of Parkhead's most famous sons lived in Westmuir Street – Baron Kirkwood of Bearsden no less! In humbler days, as David Kirkwood, he was the chief shop steward at Parkhead Forge and later one of the ILP (Independent Labour Party) MPs for Glasgow elected in 1922 (along with Bridgeton's James Maxton and Shettleston's John Wheatley). The church seen here is Parkhead Congregational.

Three of the city's 'Carnegie' libraries are still in use in the east end – Bridgeton (1906), Dennistoun (1905) and Parkhead (1906). Glasgow received a gift of £120,000 from millionaire Andrew Carnegie enabling twelve to be built. This sketch of the Parkhead Library on Tollcross Road highlights the level of architectural and ornamental detail which was their hallmark.

Springfield Road was the route to Dalmarnock and the ford across the river to Rutherglen. The northern section was known locally as Drythrapple Lone. In around 1978 this single-storey, pantile-roofed house opposite Newlands School was probably the oldest dwelling remaining in Parkhead; it was replaced by a tenement.

The ubiquitous east-ender Jack House has a ride on one of the last horse-drawn delivery carts used by A.G. Barr & Co. Most famous for its creation of our other national drink, Irn Bru, the soft drink (ginger to Glaswegians) producer has had a major presence at Parkhead since 1887.

There have been two major influences on the history of Parkhead – one being Parkhead Forge and the other Celtic Football Club. Seen here in 1938, the stadium was still a relatively modest affair compared to the modern structure which dominates the landscape. The club was founded in 1888 by the Marist Brother Walfrid at St Mary's church hall in Calton as a means to acquire funds for charitable work.

One of Celtic's greatest achievements was in winning the European Champions Cup in 1967, the first British team to do so: some of the 'Lisbon Lions' are seen here, with Bobby Murdoch held aloft at the Estadio Nacional where they had just defeated Inter Milan 2–1.

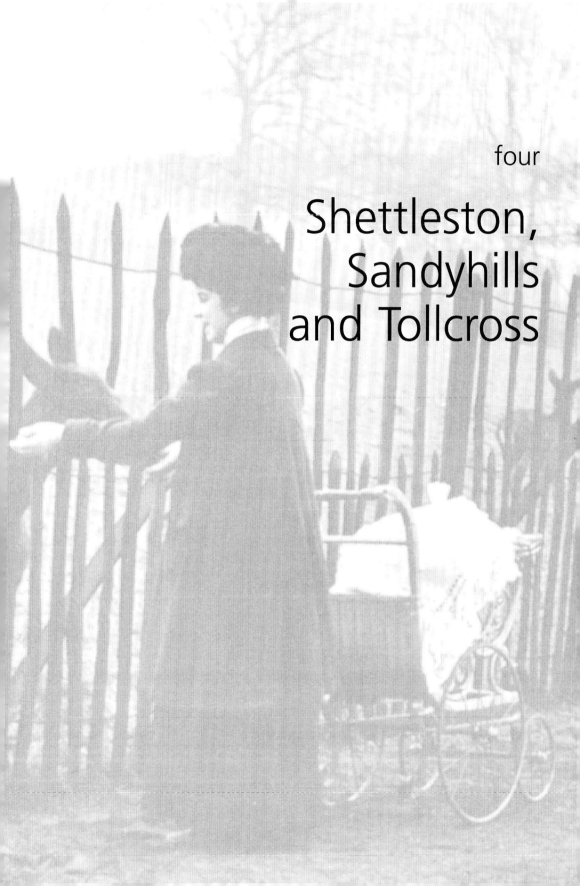

four

Shettleston, Sandyhills and Tollcross

Main Street, Shettleston — now Shettleston Road — *c.* 1910. This connected a number of small communities — Low Carntyne, Shettleston itself, Middlequarter and Eastmuir — which gradually grew and merged to form the Shettleston known today. The name is believed to be a corruption of *villam filie Sedum,* a reference to the residence of Sedin's daughter in a Papal Bull of 1179. The name 'Schedinestun' also appears in a charter granted by King Alexander II to the Bishop of Glasgow in 1226.

From the same period as above, this photograph shows Shettleston Cross. In fact, the location of the Cross is not truly known. The church is Carntyne Old Church of Scotland, which started as a Free Church in 1893.

Shettleston Old Parish church of 1901–02, at the north end of Killin Street, is only the second building to house the congregation in its 255-year history: the first church was built in 1752 in what is now Shettleston Road, but it became increasingly unsafe, especially after mining works took place beneath it, and it had to be replaced. The old churchyard walls and cemetery are preserved, situated to the east of the Kirk House pub.

This interior view shows the entry to the chancel area, with the communion table and choir stalls, which is flanked by the organ enclosure and the pulpit. It has hardly changed in over 100 years. The church has an extensive collection of stained glass and, in the vestibule, a relic of the old church – the bell. This was cast in 1663 for the Tolbooth steeple at Glasgow Cross and was presented to Shettleston in 1752.

The first St Paul's church was a small wooden structure. It was by the stone building of 1857 which was to endure for the next century. The parish was very large, as early Catholic parishes tended to be because of their scarcity, and extended to Provanmill, Baillieston and Carmyle. A very different and more modern-looking church to a design by Jack Coia replaced the traditionally Gothic architecture of the old one in 1959.

The ladies of St Barnabas' Roman Catholic church, September 2002. It takes a lot of commitment to maintain the churches within our communities, and a lot of physical work too. Churches throughout the east end owe a debt of gratitude to the legions of (mostly, it has to be said) women who undertake the more basic tasks which contribute to the inspirational surroundings that everyone benefits from. Seen here are, from left to right: Mary Augaitis, Johanna Cunningham, Mary McKean, Ada Sullivan, Margaret Rice, Patricia Neeson, Mary Deacon and Ellen Timoney.

On 9 September 1904, a meeting was held in Houston's Academy Tearoom for anyone who might be interested in forming a local 'harriers', or running, club. The outcome was the launch of a hugely successful adventure. Some of the older members who had benefited from the vision of those pioneers met in the Tearoom ninety-seven years later, to celebrate the anniversary of the foundation of the Shettleston Harriers.

Shettleston station, 1957. A line to connect Coatbridge with Glasgow was authorised in 1865 and opened five years later. It passed through Easterhouse, Shettleston and Carntyne before finally terminating in the city centre. This led to a surge in house building in Shettleston as the suburb became more easily accessible.

Above: The massed football teams of Eastbank Academy, Shettleston, 1958/59.

Left: Eastbank Academy on Shettleston Road opened in 1894 to replace Eastmuir School and became another one of a number of late Victorian schools in the east end which gained a considerable reputation for academic achievement. Although there were initial concerns that the building was 'too grand' for such a small place as Shettleston was at the time, the fears were unjustified as it quickly attained a considerable role in the community. Over the years, its popularity resulted in an ongoing expansion. The new school moved to its current site in Academy Street in 1986. In 1989, the old building provided a home for the newly created John Wheatley College. This was named after the MP who had represented the constituency from 1922-30. As part of Ramsay Macdonald's Labour Government, Wheatley was Minister of Health and led a campaign for decent housing for the working classes. A representation of the 1894 building is shown here from the cover of a school magazine of 1959, with its motto prominent: *Splendeat Lux* – 'Let Your Light Shine.'

An expectant queue of youngsters awaits admission to the Shettleston Odeon in 1955, probably for a Saturday matinée. These performances could be pretty wild events, with the usherettes' patience taxed to the limit.

The Palaceum in Hill Street (later Edrom Street), 1937. This cinema was in use from 1913-1953. No consideration of Glasgow cinemas takes place without the great 'jam jar' debate raising its head. It is undisputed that jam jars at one time could be redeemed for cash at local shops, but did cinemas ever accept them directly? This certainly happened at the 'wee' Royal in Main Street, Bridgeton, but it was not a regular practice. It seems to have been done only as an occasional special promotion by some cinemas.

Although it is now thought of as the 1920s housing scheme built by the Corporation, Sandyhills actually lay further to the east. The mid-nineteenth-century mansion house of Sandyhills estate is shown here in around 1904. The high flats which now dominate the local skyline were built on the site of the house from 1964-70.

High-rise living was a strategy adopted by Glasgow in the 1960s to deal with its housing shortage – when you can't build out, build up! Glaswegians were already accustomed to living in tenements, so multi-storey flats were seen as a reasonable progression. However, given the old mine workings which riddle the east end, relatively few were built there. The Sandyhills flats are seen here from Strowan Street in 1996.

Above: As early as 1589 it was necessary to ban the playing of 'golf, carri or shinny' in the cathedral and Blackfriars kirkyards, but the game's popularity did not diminish. Glasgow Golf Club, which was founded in 1787, has its origins on Glasgow Green and was later hosted at Alexandra Park for a period from the late nineteenth century. Sandyhills Golf Club is one of several local courses, itself having been established in 1905 on part of the Sandyhills estate. The opening of the clubhouse the following year is shown here.

Below: One of the main routes connecting Shettleston to Tollcross is Wellshot Road. A main feature in this road is Shettleston Library and public halls, built on the grounds of Tollcross Park from 1922–25.

Above: Glasgow Corporation acquired the Tollcross estate in 1897 for the use of the local population as a park. With the purchase came a mansion house, seen here in around 1910, which had been built in 1848 for the Dunlop family. The Corporation used it initially as a Children's Museum – quite an innovative idea for its time – but by 1976 it had closed down. Demolition was only avoided by the decision to allow its use as supported housing.

Below: Like other parks, Tollcross has rid itself of recreational facilities now considered to be outdated, such as the main bandstand. It has replaced them with others more in keeping with current interests: these include the Leisure Centre and a home for the Glasgow Baseball Association at Shettleston Hill. One survivor is the ever-popular Winter Gardens, shown soon after the park opened, and saved through its recent renovation.

Where it flows between Shettleston and Tollcross, Tollcross Burn has long provided a natural boundary. It is seen at it prettiest as it runs through the Glen in the park, overlooked by the mansion on its promontory, before exiting beneath Tollcross Road. It re-emerges at London Road, beyond the one-time site of Govancroft Pottery, to pass through St Peter's Cemetery at Dalbeth and on into the Clyde.

Facing directly onto Tollcross Road (known as Great Eastern Road when photographed here in around 1918) was an enclosure within the park for deer. It gave its name to a range of tenements on the opposite side of the road – Deer Park Gardens – where Jack House was born. One of the enclosure's residents – 'Old Bob'– was stuffed after his demise and became a rather sad exhibit in the Children's Museum. This area was eventually given over to use as a putting green before being developed into a highly successful Rose Garden where the annual International Rose Trials are currently held.

Tollcross as a village developed in the late eighteenth century, although the lands which provided the name were far more extensive in older times – reaching as far west as the present Eastern Necropolis (Janefield Cemetery). The small hamlets of a few houses each grew along its Main Street (shown here in around 1900) and coalesced into a community large enough to warrant the title. Farming, mining, weaving and employment in the Clyde Iron Works were the major occupations of the inhabitants. Main Street was later renamed Tollcross Road.

School would appear to be out in this 1907 photograph of Tollcross' Main Street near the intersection with Causewayside Street, at Victoria Tollcross church. The tenement at the far right has been replaced by Little Egypt youth centre. Egypt was the name of a farm in Tollcross' Calton, the surviving buildings being situated off Dalness Street. It is said to have acquired its unusual name a few centuries ago after an owner fought in Egypt with the British Army in the earlier days of Empire building.

Right: The iconic image of Tollcross, until it was demolished in 1996, was Tollcross Central Church of Scotland. Sited at the end of Church Lane, it is shown here in the late 1970s. The church was built in 1806 on Auchenshuggle land donated for the purpose and started life as a Relief congregation. Buried in an unmarked grave in the Tollcross kirkyard is William Miller, author of *Wee Willie Winkie.* Also interred at Tollcross are Stewart Murray, the first curator of Glasgow Botanic Gardens, and James Martin, town councillor and Baillie of Glasgow. The latter is commemorated by a cast-iron fountain on Glasgow Green.

Below: St Vincent's School for blind and deaf children (1920) was founded by the Daughters of Charity of St Vincent de Paul, who came to Tollcross in 1911, and who had their convent in Fullarton for a time. The Catholic Church in Tollcross is represented by St Joseph's, opened in 1976. Historically the village was part of the extensive parish of St Mary's, Calton. An old chapel school in London Road, a forerunner of the present church, was burned down in 1904. The fire was caused by sparks from a passing train.

Above: This old pantile-roofed house, photographed in 1978, sat beside Battle Burn in Corbett Street. This was Auchenshuggle land, largely centred on Easterhill Street, and part of Carmyle until recent times. The house dated from at least the early nineteenth century. It was dismantled at the instigation of the People's Palace; as it was possibly unique within the city, it had been intended to reconstruct it in Tollcross Park or Glasgow Green as a weaver's cottage, but the scheme did not come to fruition.

Below: The Miners' Institute, Corbett Street, *c.* 1957. James Dunlop of Carmyle, and later Tollcross, was considered 'the most powerful coalmaster in the west of Scotland', owning pits throughout the area in the late eighteenth century. Miners were practically slaves until 1799 and could even be exchanged between mine owners. Technology was primitive and most of the work was carried out by hand, irrespective of age or sex.

Wellshot Primary, Wellshot Road, shortly after it was opened in 1904. Where Wellshot Road reached Tollcross is thought by some to be where the Royal Burgh of Rutherglen's right to levy taxation ended, and to be the site of the original Shettleston Cross.

Braidfauld Street, towards Tollcross Main Street, c. 1911. Balmoral Terrace fronts onto the northern half of the street and remains little changed, but the rural aspect of the district continues to be lost – the greenery seen here was replaced with post-First World War tenement housing around Dunira Street. The fencing to the left enclosed a coal ree, a part of which is still occupied by a quaint wooden grocery store.

St Margaret's Tollcross Park Church of Scotland at Braidfauld Street, photographed here soon after it was built in 1900 through the efforts of John White, minister of Shettleston Parish church. Braidfauld Street was nicknamed the 'Doctors' Road', there being several medical men living there. In the mid-1960s the Corporation built the Braidfauld housing scheme at London Road, demolishing many of the older houses.

Brownlee Gardens, looking westwards towards Braidfauld Street, c. 1900. Now named Braidfauld Gardens, it was built as a middle-class suburban development most probably following the opening of the local railway station, as happened at other places in the east end. The eastern end of the Gardens met Station Road, leading up to the train station or down to the Auchenshuggle tram terminus. With the incorporation of Tollcross into Glasgow in 1912, Station Road being in line with Battle Burn, it also marked the Glasgow boundary.

Govancroft Potteries Ltd was located at 1855 London Road and operated from 1911 until 1981. The works produced a variety of wares including stoneware and jolleyed ware containers for ginger beer, jam, ink and stout. After the Second World War it concentrated on whisky jugs, many of which were made for the nearby Long John bottling plant on London Road. Here, in 1978, operators prepare to tighten up the filter press.

Mechanisation versus the craftsman – an apprentice potter developing his skills. In the pottery's early days, clay was transported as ballast in ships' holds and was trundled to the works from the docks in two-wheel carts. A trail of clay all along the route was an indication that a new consignment had arrived! The Govancroft site is now occupied by a block of housing named 'The Potteries.'

A passenger railway service opened at Tollcross in 1898, with the trams arriving not long afterwards. Previously, people walked wherever they were going or hired a horse and cart. Group excursions were more affordable – an outing to the 1904 Scottish Cup Final is seen here departing from Corbett Street.

Almost literally, the Auchenshuggle terminus on London Road proved to be the end of the line for the Glasgow trams: scheduled services ended on 2 September 1962, but the public demanded an opportunity to make a final journey, so for two more days these two No. 9 cars took passengers between Anderson Cross and 'the Shuggle' – at sixpence a fare. Shown here on 4 September at the terminus before making their way to the Dalmarnock depot, a banner proclaims, 'Goodbye Trams – For All You've Been To Us – Thanks!'

five

Dalmarnock to Daldowie

The earliest history of Dalmarnock – 'the meadow or plain abounding in bent and iris' – is strongly associated with the ford across the Clyde at this location. In medieval times it was probably used by masons who helped build the cathedral, as they travelled to and from Rutherglen, and by Mary, Queen of Scots as she fled south following her disastrous defeat at the Battle of Langside in 1568. A wooden bridge was built in 1820-21 by the Road Trustees, to be replaced in 1847-48 by another, depicted above.

The Turnpike Acts of the 1760s introduced significant improvements to the country's road system. To help pay for the construction and maintenance of roads and bridges, toll points were established at strategic points by the Road Trustees to collect a levy on users. A tollhouse, seen here in 1974, was built at on Dalmarnock Road, opposite its junction with Springfield Road, in around 1820 to collect the dues for using Dalmarnock Bridge.

Dalmarnock had been considered earlier as a potential site for a bridge linking Rutherglen to Glasgow, but lost out to Bridgeton when Rutherglen Bridge was built. The present Dalmarnock bridge, in more durable iron, steel and granite, was built in 1889-9 – the third bridge to cross the river at this point. A 'red' bus, from the Lanarkshire side, crosses the bridge in 1975. Once over it could only allow passengers to alight, but could not pick any up within Glasgow. The reverse conditions applied on the return journey.

A triumph of Victorian engineering in the making – the laying of the foundation stone of the present Dalmarnock Bridge on 11 October 1889. In the background is the temporary wooden bridge which had been put in place for use while the works were being undertaken. A memorial plaque on the bridge informs passers-by that the construction was a joint effort between the City of Glasgow, the Lower and Middle Wards of Lanark and the Royal Burgh of Rutherglen.

Springfield Road looking north from Dalmarnock Road, *c.* 1900. In the distance is William Miller's Springfield Dyeworks. The road was known as the 'Black Road' in the early 1830s but took its formal name from the Springfield area. This name also attached to Springfield House and Springfield Farm.

Dalmarnock Road from Swanston Street looking towards Bridgeton Cross in around 1909, illustrating the predominance of the horse and cart for transport. This was the approximate site of the boundary between Bridgeton and Dalmarnock, which was commonly taken to be Bartholomew Street.

Sunnybank Street, 1974, towards Dalmarnock Parish church. The uniform ranks of tenements which were as typical of Dalmarnock as anywhere else in Glasgow did not arise by accident; they resulted from the accumulation of building controls imposed by the land's feudal superiors over the years. Eventually, these restrictions became so elaborate and detailed that only buildings of a very similar design could be constructed. The word tenement derives from the Latin *tenementum* meaning a parcel of land.

Ardenlea Street towards Our Lady of Fatima church, 1974. This was the birthplace of Dalmarnock's most famous son, Kenny Dalglish, who played for Celtic and was later player-manager at Liverpool FC. The street runs through the heart of the smaller of the two old Dalmarnock estates, this one belonging to the Waddrop family for about 400 years. Their Dalmarnock House was also known as Springfield House.

The high flats at Dalmarnock provided a vantage point in 1974 for this view of the power station. The generation of electricity was only one of the major utilities which were concentrated in this district, the others over time including a gas works, a water works and a sewage plant. The power station was mostly constructed on the larger of the two Dalmarnock estates between 1920 and 1926 and later extended. It too was swept away in the huge changes to the inner east end which accompanied the ten-year GEAR program, the latter being commemorated in Dalmarnock's Gear Terrace.

The Dalmarnock Picture House in Nuneaton Street operated from 1922-1959, changing its name to the Plaza in 1945. The Dalmarnock is credited with the earliest local showing of the first full-length talking feature film, *The Singing Fool*, in 1929. The late 1950s saw the closure of many cinemas as the popularity of television grew. The Plaza was derelict by 1974.

Above: In 2004 the church of Our Lady of Fatima was unexpectedly closed, its last service being held on 28 January. The parish was absorbed into that of the Sacred Heart, from whence it had originated in 1950. It had fallen victim to the ongoing depopulation and general deterioration of the whole area which has continued apace, despite the efforts of GEAR. Behind it, here in 1975, are the high flats in the Allan Street area, themselves only recently demolished. The church was taken down in late 2006.

Right: Dalmarnock Parish church, 1974. This fairly typical example of late Victorian church architecture was built in 1866 and taken down in 1977 as part of a street-widening programme. It was located on Springfield Road almost opposite to Sunnybank Street. The congregation joined with that of Calton Old Parish church in Helenvale Street to form Calton Parkhead church.

Above: The Clyde loops towards Springfield Road, as seen from the Dalmarnock multi-storey flats, 1974. In the foreground are the Dalmarnock Paper Mills leading towards Riverside Secondary School. In the far distance are the 1967-69 Helenvale Street high flats, with Celtic Park just visible to their left. If Glasgow's bid for the 2014 Commonwealth Games proves successful, much of this space will be the site of the Athletes' Village.

Below: Riverside Secondary School; Riverside opened in 1933. It is believed to have been built with a view to conversion into hospital accommodation during wartime – possibly a lesson learned from the First World War of 1914-18. When built it was considered to be 'state of the art', with wide corridors and spacious classrooms, but it was plagued by subsidence from the beginning, no doubt the price it paid for its proximity to the river.

London Road stretches off westwards from its junction with Springfield Road, as seen from Helenvale high flats, *c.* 1978. The council housing in the upper left quadrant of this photograph has all now been demolished. Beyond this, the remains of the workshops of Sir William Arrol's Dalmarnock works can just be seen. Arrol's had specialised in bridge building, with its more famous projects including the rail bridges spanning the Forth and Tay, and Tower Bridge in London.

London Road east of Helenvale high flats, *c.* 1978. The background is dominated by the Clyde Iron Works/Clydebridge Steelworks complex. London Road, now a modern dual carriageway, is thought to have started as a rough country lane which became established as a more major route out of Glasgow in the late eighteenth century when the Clyde Iron Works was built.

Belvidere Hospital, *c.* 1978. When an epidemic of relapsing fever broke out in 1870, Glasgow's hospitals were overwhelmed and emergency accommodation was needed. Belvidere estate was purchased and temporary pavilions were speedily constructed. Recognising the benefits of having a permanent facility on its outskirts, the city decided that Belvidere should continue to be used as a fever and smallpox hospital. In 1900 it even dealt with an outbreak of bubonic plague. Its role changed over the years until it was finally closed in 1999.

Cleanliness was of vital importance to the work undertaken at Belvidere. A wash house was on site and a member of staff is seen here passing laundry from a disinfectant tank through a mangle, *c.* 1914. The work at the hospital was tiring, innovatory and dangerous. Many staff died caring for their charges. These sacrifices were acknowledged in a memorial erected by the Corporation at Sandymount Cemetery.

Above: 'Harvey's Dyke' by Robert Carrick. Not the first or last landowner to try to restrict public access to the Clydeside, but certainly one of the most notorious, was 'Lang Tam' Harvey. Three years after purchasing the Westthorn estate in 1819, he built a formidable wall – with a guard room and even a small cannon at one stage – across the footpath and down into the river. When a Dalmarnock landowner tried to do likewise, public outrage spilled over into a riot. The Dalmarnock obstruction was destroyed: the crowd then moved upriver and tried to do the same to Harvey's dyke. They were prevented from completing their work by a troop of soldiers summoned by Harvey. The dyke was rebuilt, but the case was taken to court by a committee of representatives from the affected villages. Finally, in July 1828, the House of Lords declared the footpath to be a right of way for all time, and Harvey was required to remove his wall.

Below: A view upriver from the site of Harvey's dyke. The amenity of the Clydeside has been preserved and made more accessible in recent years by the development of the Clyde Walkway, which now runs from central Glasgow to New Lanark.

The offices of John Dewar & Sons Ltd's bonded warehouse site and bottling plant at Westthorn front onto London Road. The site is still known locally as 'the Long John' despite the changes in ownership which have taken place since this photograph was taken in around 1978. The warehouses are partly owned by Beam Global. In 1953, the majority of the Westthorn estate was acquired by Long John International which built warehouses for whisky storage and, in 1969, the bottling hall. This continued a connection with the whisky trade, from Lang Tam Harvey to Long John MacDonald. At one time, from the banks of the river, the empty casks stored on the grassy slopes between the warehouses could be seen. However, the site has been flooded several times. A spectacular instance occurred in 1985 when the river overflowed. The embankment was breached by the company to allow flood water to recede but the river caused this breach to enlarge, allowing many empty casks to flow into the river and on downstream. The Clyde Port Authority had to put a boom across the river to catch them. Over the years additional barriers of rubble have been raised to create more impenetrable defences to the river's waters.

Left: The bottling hall, *c.* 1980.

Opposite above: Dalbeth – Gaelic for 'a field or meadow covered in birchwood' – remains as the core of an older property on the banks of the Clyde, paralleling Tollcross on its northern boundary. By the eighteenth century it had been broken down into separate estates at Springbank, Belvidere, Westthorn, Dalbeth itself, and Easterhill. Each had its own mansion house, that of Dalbeth shown here in around 1878. One notable resident was Thomas Hopkirk, an ardent botanist whose Dalbeth collection provided the nucleus for creating Glasgow's Botanic Gardens.

Below: The Good Shepherd complex at Dalbeth in 1958. The estate was purchased by the Catholic Church in 1850, with the Good Shepherd Sisters residing there until 1949. Facilities eventually included a Magdalene Asylum and separate reformatories for boys and girls.

The Presbytery building of the Good Shepherd sits atop its elevated site, facing towards the Clyde, c. 1974. The Good Shepherd church itself was built in 1902 and demolished along with other buildings when the parish was closed in 1975. The associated St Peter's Cemetery remains in use by the city's Catholic population. Buried here is the Shettleston MP John Wheatley, who died in 1930.

Established in 1982 as Glasgow's first Community Nature Park, Auchenshuggle Wood was formed on the lands of Fullarton to preserve woodland considered to be a unique resource in the east end, and to provide a haven for indigenous species of tree such as oak, ash, hazel and rowan and a variety of native flowers. That same year, children from St James' Primary in Bridgeton helped with planting at the wood.

Carmyle Avenue   *Carmyle*

Published by Wm. Cowie, Carmyle

Carmyle has always been an isolated community and seems more so since the extension of the M74 through its northern borders. The district extended into what would now be considered Tollcross, with the two communities becoming even more closely intertwined in 1810 when the Dunlops of Carmyle purchased the Tollcross estate. Carmyle Avenue, seen in 1906, was the main route between the villages.

CARMYLE AVENUE.

Carmyle Avenue continues across London Road into Carmyle proper. The community's name is believed to derive from two Gaelic words – *Cair-mol* or *Cathair-Maol* – meaning 'the bare town' or the 'bare rounded rock.' The fertile riverbank areas are thought to have been cleared of forest for cultivation very early on, and probably gave it a relatively barren appearance in comparison with the surrounding countryside.

Main Street, Carmyle

Main Street, Carmyle later became South Carmyle Avenue, and led down past the only tenements – named 'the buildings' by locals – to the riverside. The lower end of the Avenue is still flooded by the Clyde on a regular basis. It was probably the mud deposits from these floods which made the land so fertile in the first place, and encouraged the monks who initially farmed it in the twelfth century.

Balmoral Drive, Carmyle, c. 1911. That Carmyle was owned by the Catholic Church provides the source of its entry into the historical record. It was gifted by the Bishop of Glasgow, Herbert, from his extensive domains to the Cistercian monks of Newbattle Abbey in the mid-twelfth century. In time it passed into the ownership of the Hutcheson family, whose descendants were the founders of the grammar school and hospital in Glasgow which bear their name.

By necessity, farming existed cheek-by-jowl with mining and other industrial activities until fairly recently throughout the eastern districts, Carmyle included. Some farm workers are seen here at River Road on their way to a day in the fields.

Rab Haddow in London Road at Auchenshuggle delivering bales of finished material for James Park & Co. of Carmyle. Park owned the Bleachfield works in River Road which had been in operation from 1741. Traditionally, material such as gingham, poplin and linen would be laid out on grassland to bleach naturally in the daylight, but by the twentieth century mechanical and chemical processes had long since taken over. Materials would arrive at the works from as far afield as Manchester and Nottingham, and 'finishing' included cleaning and undertaking any stitching work necessary, such as hemming handkerchiefs. The works closed in 1961, and was eventually demolished. The Ardargie estate was built on the site.

Above: The Catholic Church re-established its physical presence in Carmyle in 1954 when priests from neighbouring St Joseph's in Tollcross used the local Welfare Hall for services. This was part of the process of establishing the parish of St Joachim's later the same year. Through the physical efforts of the parishioners, the Carmyle Mains Steading farm in River Road (currently the Banks Bar) was converted into the first church of the new parish by the following year. This was then used until the present St Joachim's in Inzievar Terrace was opened for use in 1957.

Left: Carmyle Parish Church of Scotland in Carmyle Avenue has its roots in the activities of the Tollcross Free church congregation in the area from 1896. This resulted in a temporary 'iron' church being built in 1902, by which time the Free and United Presbyterian Churches had unified to become the United Free Church. Only five years later, the stone church still in use today was built. When Carmyle's industrial targets were attacked by the Luftwaffe during the Second World War, the church had to be repaired after it sustained blast damage. It also underwent major renovations more recently. Since 1978, the church has been linked with Kenmuir Mount Vernon church in London Road.

Above: The Clyde's Mill power station across the river in Cambuslang dominated the Carmyle landscape from 1916 until it was demolished. One enterprising Carmyle woman kept a boat and would ferry workmen to and from the opposite bank. Despite its seemingly rural aspect these days, industrial activity figured very early in Carmyle's history. The monks were known to mine local coal and a flour mill was built at the riverside in around 1268. The late eighteenth century saw coal mining develop as a major source of employment, with many pits being dug in the area. This, plus the availability of iron-stone, led to the foundation of the Clyde Iron Works in 1786.

Right: The lesson of Tam Harvey was lost on some local landowners, who again tried to block the pathway along the banks of the river in 1891. The villagers successfully asserted their rights to free access and commemorated their victory by subscribing to the erection of a drinking fountain. The cast-iron fountain, made at the Saracen Foundry, stood near River Road from 1892 until 1957. The villagers were very proud of their fountain, but for some unknown reason it vanished in 1957. Some local folk believe that it was stolen for its scrap value. It is hoped that the memorial will be replaced by something suitable one day.

A group of workers at the thirteenth-century meal mill. Little is known of the history of the mill although it still seems to have been operating until the 1920s. The man with the shotgun was not a gamekeeper – his job was to control the rat population.

Daldowie is now best known as the location of the crematorium, built in 1950 on what had been yet another of the impressive riverside estates. Among its more notable owners from 1724 to 1825 were the Bogle family. In medieval times, this family had rented extensive areas of land from the Church in Daldowie, Carmyle and Shettleston and they subsequently became important landowners. In 1999 the only vestige of the old estate was the impressive red sandstone dovecot built by the Bogles in 1745. While modern dovecots, which seem to spring up on any vacant site in the east end, are concerned with the breeding and racing of pigeons, the traditional dovecots were created to provide one of the few sources of fresh food during the long winter months. By 1999, the estate around it was a sewage works and the dovecot was in a serious state of dereliction. Through the efforts of a variety of agencies in partnership, it was dismantled and transported a kilometre to the east. The dovecot was rebuilt and restored on a landscaped site at Hamilton Road where it can now be accessed by the public.

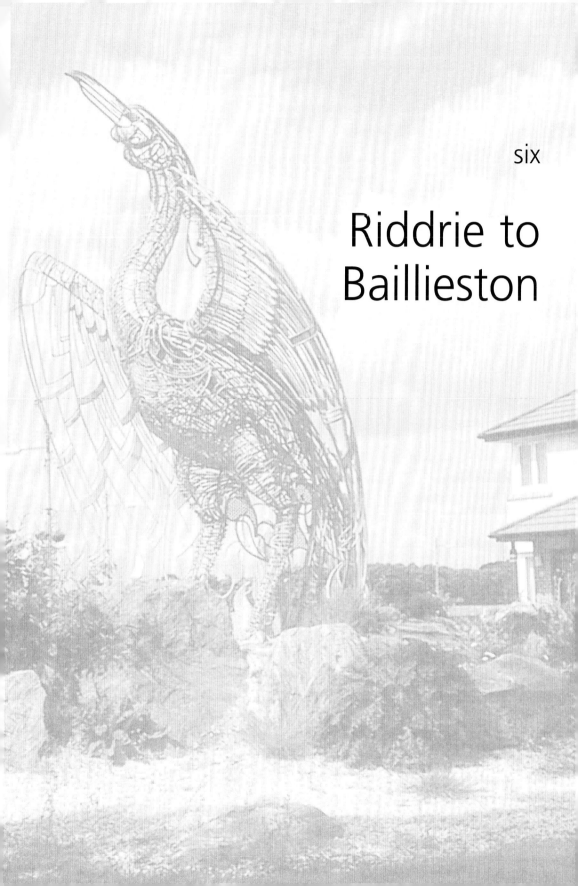

six

Riddrie to
Baillieston

Kennyhill House, 1916. The Kennyhill estate was at the junction of the present Alexandra Parade and Cumbernauld Road. Part of its lands went to make up Alexandra Park and, from 1919, the Riddrie and Kennyhill housing scheme. The mansion house was acquired by the city and converted into a school for children with special needs. The building has since been replaced by a new school which continues to provide a valuable community service.

The housing scheme was one of the first ventures into public housing provision by Glasgow's housing department. Faced with a tremendous lack of affordable and decent housing for the majority of its citizens, this effort was presented as building housing 'fit for heroes' coming back from the trenches of the First World War. In fact, the strategy was to lure the more affluent working and lower-middle classes from the inner-city areas to free up housing stock there for others. The tenements shown here in around 1930 were in Don Street.

Tay Crescent, Riddrie

Construction lasted from 1919-1927, during which more than a thousand houses were built. The housing mix was of tenements to the south, with terraced and semi-detached houses to the north. Tay Crescent, here seen probably post-Second World War, was one of two crescents built across from Barlinnie Prison.

Barlinnie and Officer's Quarters, Riddrie.

Built between the years of 1880-86, and seen here in the 1930s, Barlinnie quickly became a general prison for the whole of Scotland. Its more notorious inmates have included Peter Manual and Jimmy Boyle. The first was hanged there: the second was a success story arising from the prison's innovative Special Unit. A lesser known inmate of the 'Bar-L' was Charging Thunder, a Lakota Sioux and member of Buffalo Bill's show while it was at Dennistoun. He spent some time in the prison for assaulting a fellow showman.

Smithycroft Secondary in Riddrie was one of the beneficiaries of the Public Private Partnership initiative which sought to rationalise secondary school provision in Glasgow and rebuild older schools. The entrance to the old Smithycroft is seen here in 2002 shortly before it was demolished. The school was built in 1967-75, with its most notable feature being a circular main classroom block: this was an architectural feature unique to the entire country, and was affectionately known by pupils as the 'doughnut.'

Glasgow was a target for bombers during the Second World War and in anticipation of air raids, which materialised during 1940-41, thousands of shelters were built all over the city. In tenement back courts these tended to take the form of communal brick and concrete structures, now probably all gone. Where gardens were available, individuals could have an Anderson shelter. A surprising number of these can still be seen in gardens all over the east end, serving a variety of purposes. The one shown here is in Ness Street, 2000.

The Monkland Canal was started in 1770 to a design by James Watt and was built in stages as finance became available. Taking almost twenty-five years to complete, it eventually ran from Calderbank in the east to Port Dundas in the west. Its purpose was to bring cheap coal from the mines of Lanarkshire to meet the growing demands of the city, and since its route passed through Easterhouse, Garthamlock and Riddrie the pits there could also access it. This scene at Riddrie in 1925 shows the canal where it was bridged to carry Cumbernauld Road.

In its later days, the once highly successful canal was abandoned and fell into a state of dereliction, as can be seen here in 1955 where it runs through Riddrie towards the gas holders at Blochairn. The canal within Glasgow was basically eliminated with the construction of the M8 motorway, which followed the original route established by the canal's engineers.

Above: Set in spacious grounds to support therapeutic farm work and recreational activities for the patients, Gartloch Hospital was built on the Gartloch estate from 1890 onwards. The main structure followed the Victorian Glasgow convention of the time for asylums to be of an apparently fortified massiveness, remote, built atop hills and dominating the surrounding land in which they were placed. The hospital closed in 1996, but the beautiful setting adjacent to Bishop Loch has proven very attractive to developers who have since built Gartloch Village on the site, converting some of the hospital buildings to housing use.

Below: The Molendinar Burn flows westwards into Glasgow from Hogganfield Loch. Hogganfield and Frankfield lochs, as part of the lands of Provan, were purchased by Glasgow in 1667 to ensure a drinking water supply from the Molendinar and use of the burn as a water source to power the town mills. The lands were sold off in 1729 but 300 acres of Ruchazie and Frankfield were bought back in 1920, of which 93 acres were used to create Hogganfield Park. A bird sanctuary within the park has gained Local Nature Reserve status as an important site for migrating and wintering water fowl.

By the late nineteenth century, Italian immigrants to the city were selling ice-cream from a variety of vehicles. This example shows what has now become a familiar sight in city parks, in this instance at Hogganfield Loch.

Sumburgh Street, Cranhill in 1997. The fleet of vans selling ice cream in customers' own containers, as well as a variety of other provisions, grew with the building of the peripheral housing estates. They were a life-line to those who moved to the new houses only to find that there were few, if any, local shops. Even today, options can be quite limited. There was a darker side to the vans. Increased competition, and possibly drug dealing, led to the notorious 'Ice Cream Wars' of the 1980s, which culminated in the tragic death of six members of the Doyle family in Ruchazie as the result of an arson attack on their home.

Shettleston Harriers coach Alex Naylor in the late 1960s puts some young champions through their paces at Cranhill's cinder track; John Cherry, Alan Gibson, Bobby McLean, John Mulvey and Alan Roberts. The unpopular post-war houses in the background have now almost all been demolished and replaced.

With falling school rolls, the east end has lost many of its secondary schools, including John Street, Cranhill and St Gregory's. Lochend and St Leonard's Secondaries in Lochend Road are shown here in 1998 just as St Leonard's was being demolished. It was replaced by a new St Benedict's Primary. Lochend was part of the school renewal programme funded by the Public Private Partnership initiative and was completely rebuilt.

It seems remarkable to be able to capture all of Easterhouse within two photographs, but this is what was essentially achieved here in the years just before the First World War when the sprawling housing scheme of that name had not even been thought of. This small mining community sat beside a bridge spanning the Monkland Canal, and stretched along the route leading south to Swinton.

Sandwiched between the M8 motorway and the Glasgow to Airdrie railway line, old Easterhouse is now something of a backwater with few of its early buildings still intact. Any resources it once had were swamped by the population equivalent to a large Scottish town, rising to 56,000 by the 1960s, suddenly appearing on its doorstep from 1954 onwards with little in the way of any community facilities of its own.

Above: St John Ogilvie, Easterhouse, 2003. Opened in 1957 as the Blessed John Ogilvie, it underwent its name change when Ogilvie was canonised by Pope Paul VI in 1976. This followed the recovery of a local man, John Fagin, from terminal cancer. The healing was deemed to be miraculous and attributable to the saint. Above the altar is a depiction of Ogilvie's martyrdom by hanging at Glasgow Cross in 1615.

Some workers making their way home from Queenslie Industrial Estate in 1962. Queenslie was the name given to an area once known as Easter Cowhuncholie (Cranhill being Wester Cowhuncholie). By the late eighteenth century some owners of newly formed country estates discarded the old Gaelic names in preference for what they considered to be more civilised names. Several industrial estates were built in the east end of the city following the Second World War to provide ready-made factory space. This was to encourage light engineering works to replace the heavy engineering industries which were in decline. Two of these estates were built at Carntyne and Queenslie and are still in operation. The Carntyne Estate was built beside a railway station and was more easily accessible for any workforce, but Queenslie was more remote. Although it opened in 1948, this problem was not easily resolved until the population of the local housing estates grew from the 1950s onwards.

Right: British Olivetti was one of the first businesses to move into the estate. The 1950s was a time of considerable expansion for the typewriter manufacturer and they soon employed more than 900 staff. This 1955 photograph shows a typewriter being assembled.

Opposite below: Possibly the oldest house in Glasgow, Provan Hall in Auchenlea Park was the country residence for the Prebend of Barlanark, a territory allocated to one of the canons of Glasgow Cathedral in medieval times to provide an income. Barlanark's town residence was Provand's Lordship near the cathedral. It is truly remarkable that both these buildings have survived since the fifteenth century. The last canon, William Baillie, secured Barlanark's transfer to Thomas Baillie – possibly his son – at the Reformation.

Springboig Road, seen here in 1906, forms part of a route which rises steeply from Shettleston and the Clyde valley to its enclosing hills, the moorland heights containing Hogganfield, Frankfield and Bishop Lochs. The one time land of Springboig Farm is traversed by the Camlachie Burn and is now mostly given over to Corporation housing of varying dates and styles. Bertrohill Road is in the distance.

Lightburn Hospital on Carntyne Road was opened in 1896 as an Infectious Diseases Hospital/Fever Hospital. Apart from two staff houses facing onto the road, all of the other buildings were demolished in 1964 and replaced by a modern hospital which now provides specialist services to the older people of east Glasgow. The Scots author, A.J. Cronin, was appointed resident superintendent at the hospital for a time. Among his works was the creation of the central character of television's *Dr Finlay's Casebook*.

Football is not the only sport enjoyed in the east end. This run up Springboig Road, or 'metal brae' as it was also known, as part of a 1954 Shettleston Harriers club trial has Joe McGhee leading the field, closely followed by Eddie Bannon, Clark Wallace, Jimmy Thompson, Hugo Fox, Walter McFarlane and John Eadie.

Also continuing to go from strength to strength is the Easterhouse Amateur Weightlifting Club. It was started in an Easterhouse close in 1986 by Alex Richardson in response to frustration at a lack of resources. By 1996 its commemorative booklet, 'Stairway to Success', could record a remarkable listing of achievements at major events worldwide. It continues, as part of the Gladiator Program, to be one of the most successful in the UK.

Carntyne Farm, *c.* 1920s. For a very long time Carntyne, along with parts of Dalmarnock, was the property of the Gray family. The most notable feature of their estate appears to have been the almost limitless deposits of coal which were mined by the family from 1600 to 1875. The Carntyne pits were a major source of supply for Glasgow despite their being constantly troubled by flooding.

Carntyne Station opened in 1870. With easier access to the Lanarkshire coalfields facilitated by the Monkland Canal and the railways, the Carntyne coal became less crucial to Glasgow. The continuing problems with flooding finally made it more economically sensible to feu land for building rather than continue to mine the coal. The Carntyne colliery was finally abandoned in 1875. The quaint Victorian station house, seen here in 1956, has been replaced by an unmanned and functional concrete and steel shelter.

Mount Vernon, 1910. Historical accounts usually report that Windyedge was renamed Mount Vernon by its new owner, George Buchanan, following a similar change of name to the first US President's (George Washington's) family home. However, local historian Robert Murray has recently demonstrated that this cannot have been the case. The estate was renamed by an earlier proprietor, Robert Boyd, in honour of Admiral Edward Vernon in 1742, at least a year before the US estate acquired the name.

Glasgow has many small enclaves of Victorian villas around old railways station, the result of early commuting becoming an alternative to city living. Mount Vernon North was one of the stations around which the suburban area of Mount Vernon grew. The station closed for passenger service the same year this photograph was taken, in 1955.

BANK CORNER, GARROWHILL.

Garrowhill was identified as a suitable site for a new, experimental Garden Estate as early as 1923 but building was not begun until 1934; it was then interrupted by the Second World War. This view of Barrachnie Road at Baillieston Road leading into Garrowhill, previously the lands of Barrachnie, dates from the post-war years. Little has changed, although the Bank of Scotland has replaced the British Linen Bank of the photograph's title.

COMMUNITY CENTRE, GARROWHILL.

Maxwell Drive, Garrowhill, *c.* 1964. From Douglas Drive it rises to the hill from which the area derives its name, and which still continues as its green heart; a vestige of the old estate. Mure Memorial Church of Scotland, built from 1936, sits atop the hill, only just visible here through the trees. Community involvement and creative leisure were guiding principles for the creation of the estate. The community centre seen here is still in use, as is the adjacent Garrowhill Bowling Club of 1937.

The sculptor Andy Scott has undertaken commissions for a broad variety of clients worldwide and many of his works are on public display throughout his native city. The figure of a phoenix is a symbol of regeneration and it is used in this manner in Easterhouse to signify the rejuvenation of the area in which it sits. This representation, characteristically in galvanised steel, was made for the Blairtummock Residents' Association in 2001. It stands in a landscaped area at the junction of Aberdalgie Road and Easterhouse Road.

Probably one of the most frequently observed sculptural figures in the Glasgow landscape, seen by the thousands of motorists who drive along the M8 motorway every day, is Scott's 'Heavy Horse.' Sited on the outskirts of Easterhouse, in Glasgow Business Park, it was made for Arlington Property Developments in 1997. The Clydesdale horse stands 4.5m high atop a mound, mere yards from the motorway.

Baillieston Main Street looking east, with Rhinsdale United Free church to the left. *c.* 1900. Baillieston is a community of fairly recent origin; it is unlikely that it existed in any significant form prior to 1795. Many similar centres of population were springing up during the late eighteenth century, initially mainly composed of hand-loom weavers. With the opening of the Monkland Canal, and the market for coal at Glasgow becoming far more accessible, mining became the principal occupation of many of the inhabitants.

Historically, Crosshill predates Baillieston, but was gradually absorbed by its neighbour. Its name suggests a closer connection with the one-time owners of the entire area from the mid-twelfth century, the Cistercian monks of Newbattle Abbey, and it was perhaps the site of a roadside shrine or other holy place at one time.

Muirhead Road on a cold winter's day, *c.* 1904. It is thought that Baillieston's late arrival on the historical scene may have been due to the geography of the area, it being largely moorland. The locale abounds with names indicating the waterlogged nature of the ground (Ellismuir, Rhindmuir and Muirside). Farming was not really possible until land management techniques were developed, which allowed it to be improved sufficiently for cultivation. Even Baillieston's coal pits were notorious for flooding.

A standard tram prepares for its return journey to Anderston Cross via Parkhead in 1959. The trams came to Baillieston in 1910 and this spot, at the beginning of Glasgow Road, is still in use as a bus stop.

A blacksmith's forge at Baillieston, *c.* 1930. The centuries-long dependence upon the horse, whether for pulling a cart or a plough, for warfare or for pleasure, ensured the blacksmith's place in society. With the advent of trains, trams and then the car, the need for his skills declined to the extent that forges are now few and far between.

'Tattie howking', or picking potatoes, at Findlay's Nurseries in Springhill, *c.* 1945. The seemingly relentless spread of new housing estates continues to swallow up the remaining farmland in Glasgow's eastern districts. Farming communities were among the earliest types of settlement. This certainly seems to be case at Springhill where farm labourers at Springhill Farm uncovered evidence in 1936 of an Iron-Age burial site.